FIBERARTS DESIGN BOOK FOUR

Dedicated to Betty Park

Dust jacket: Detail of Stick Construction Number 4 *by Barbara Allen.*
Hand blown paper, linen, sticks, pastels, pigments; 28 by 28 inches.
Photo: Thomas Mezzanotte.

Published in 1991 by Lark Books
50 College Street
Asheville, North Carolina, U.S.A. 28801

Library of Congress Cataloging-in-Publication Data:

Fiberarts Design Book IV / edited by Nancy Orban
    p.   cm.
    Includes index.
    ISBN 0-937274-56-9 : $29.95
    1. Textile crafts.   2. Fiberwork   I. Orban, Nancy, 1938-
    II. Fiberarts.   III. Title: Fiberarts design book 4.
    IV. Title: Fiberarts design book four.
    TT699.F524   1991
    746--dc20   91-11695
                               CIP

10 9 8 7 6 5 4 3 2 1

Printed in Hong Kong by Oceanic Graphic Printing

FIBERARTS DESIGN BOOK FOUR

EDITED BY NANCY ORBAN

Lark Books

FIBERARTS DESIGN BOOK FOUR

EDITOR:
Nancy Orban

DESIGN/ART DIRECTOR:
Rob Pulleyn

PRODUCTION:
Sandra Montgomery
Elaine Thompson
Dougal Bailey

VALUABLE ASSISTANCE:
Ann Batchelder   Marcia Winters
Dawn Cusick   Pat Wald
Jacqueline Corbett Geri Camarda
Carol Taylor   Laurel Winters

PUBLISHER:
Rob Pulleyn

TABLE OF CONTENTS

INTRODUCTION

This fourth edition of the Fiberarts Design Book documents the developments in the textile art field that have taken place in the last four years.

The Design Book series, started in 1980, has been instrumental in documenting contemporary fiber work over the last 15 years. New directions in fiber can be more clearly traced with each edition, while fads come and go.

In the last decade and a half, we have seen the ascendancy of surface design (warp painting, fabric painting, fiber dyeing), the enduring strength of quilting and tapestry, and the continued fascination with needlework, basketry, handmade paper, and wearables. In addition, many fiber artists have had an ongoing fascination with mixed media constructions.

With each edition, we note the growing aesthetic sophistication, greater technical assurance, and developing independence of artistic vision. More specifically in this fourth edition, we were struck by a larger color palette and the frequent incorporation of serious social/political commentary as well as humorous personal messages through narrative imagery.

Fiberarts Design Book Four also dramatically points to a growing international fiber network. The first Design Book included work from eight countries, while this book includes artists from 24 countries. There are as many artists from Czechoslovakia in this Design Book, for example, as there were countries represented in the last edition.

This expanding international community of fiber artists encourages a greater exchange of technical information and artistic passion. As one small byproduct of international sharing, this edition has been published simultaneously in English and Japanese and will be distributed to readers in six continents.

The last ten years have seen a dramatic acceptance of fiber and other craft media by the "fine" arts world. More and more prestigious galleries and museums are mounting major exhibitions of fiber art. Some will argue this is simply the result of gallery owners looking for aesthetic merchandise that is more reasonably priced than paintings. Others argue that it has taken a decade for contemporary fiber art to produce a substantial number of artists who have developed significant bodies of work for exhibition.

While artists who work in fiber prefer to be known as artists first, fiber artists, quilters, or tapestrymakers second, they choose to work in this medium because it adds something—a tactile dimension, a sculptural quality, an intensity of color—to their artistic vision. With increased confidence, there also is less rebellion against textile traditions and, in fact, there is an increased sense of fiber history in many contemporary works.

Fiber is still a small field in the world of art, but the passion for fiber burns brightly. Sewers proudly display bumper stickers emblazoned with messages such as "Whoever dies with the most fabric wins," weavers hoard yarn beyond any future need simply because yarn is beautiful to look at and to touch, and embroiderers can find an old tube of beads that will keep them happy all week.

In other words, fiber artists love the *stuff*, the material, that defines their media, and have begun to develop a vocabulary that does not immediately relate to paint or metal or clay. There is a growing network of galleries, museums, journals, and critics devoted to the fiber field that helps explain, display, sell, argue, fund, and inspire.

Only a small percentage of the artists in fiber make their living working full time in the field. For the majority, their driving passion is compromised by other important realities. Some of the artists in this book are world renowned, the subjects of heavy coffee table books and major museum exhibitions. Many more are well known in the fiber field, commanding respect by colleagues and collectors and frequently exhibiting their work. Most of the artists, however, work quietly, removed from the concerns of agents and press releases; yet their work is no less worthy or significant.

Related to this, we must admit our pleasure in presenting the well known and the unknown side by side. It is very satisfying to watch the unknowns become discovered through these Design Books, to have collectors write and ask for addresses or to see artists a year or two later announce their own exhibitions.

This series of books is a celebration of the diversity, passion, quality, and joy of the fiber arts. As in the past, the fourth edition is the result of many months of preparation. Thousands of slides were anonymously reviewed with three loosely constructed criteria in mind: artistic integrity, technical expertise, and innovative ideas (read: "we liked it"). For the sake of organization, the works have been grouped, sometimes uncomfortably, into chapters.

We hope that, like *Fiberarts* magazine itself, this book will bring recognition to its contributors and encouragement and inspiration to its readers. We invite you to sit back in a comfortable chair, put on a favorite piece of music and dig in. Thank you all.

The Fiberarts Staff

Linda Hutchins
Rubicon
Tapestry; linen, wool, goat hair;
38 by 37 inches.
Photo: Bill Bachhuber

A

Christine Laffer

Governments Take Hostages

Tapestry; wool, linen, rayon;
38 by 38 inches.
Photo: Jacques Cressaty

*Free expression of ideas and
opinions can be perceived as
threatening by any established
government, however secure.
The speaker may or may not
understand the suppression of
his voice, but the severity of offi-
cial repression remains a life-
altering force.*

B

Peter Harris

Kapital

Tapestry; wool, linen; 48 by 64
inches.

C

Ruth Scheuer

Urban Relics: Rent Apart In

Tapestry, rubber stamp
printing; wool, cotton, ink;
14 by 18 inches.
Photo: Elijah Cobb

*Coptic tapestry fragments and
Samuel Beckett's poetry inspired the piece. Both express
fragmentation, one visually,
one verbally.*

D

Aase Vaslow

Relentless Serenity

Woven tapestry; wool, cotton;
25 by 16½ inches.

A

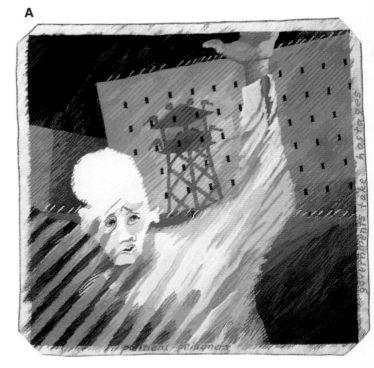

B

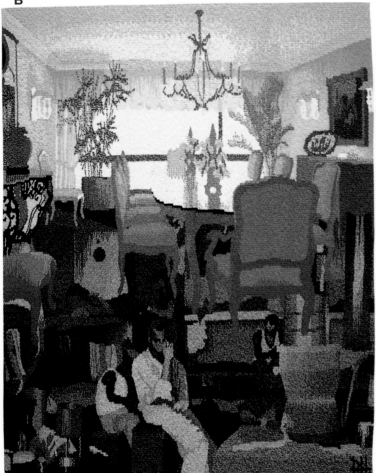

C

D

E

Sally Oswald Hands

Charles & Di Attend a Rock Concert

Woven tapestry; wool; 42 by 36 inches.
Photo: W. Zehr

I designed this after I went to a Rod Stewart concert.

F

Teresa Graham Salt

Window

Tapestry; silk, metallic threads, photo transfer; 7 by 8½ inches.

I'm influenced by pop culture. I want to amuse myself and the viewer and also comment on the state of my life.

E

F

A

Soyoo Hyunjoo Park

Racing

Gobelin tapestry; cotton,
polyester, silk; 35 by 24 inches.

*I wanted an image of speed.
By using similar colors in the
Hatcher, I can achieve subtle
color gradations, and by using
dissimilar colors, I get an effect
very similar to that of photographed moving objects.*

B

Joyce Hulbert

Untitled

Tapestry; dyed wool, silk, linen,
cotton; 36 by 36 inches.

*By dyeing my yarns I achieve a
personal palette that addresses
both the content of my imagery
and the symbolic capacity of
color.*

C

Julien Englebert BAL

Fish Caught in the Morning

Tapestry; wool; 1½ by 1⅕ m.

A

B

C

D

E

F

A

Deann Joy Rubin

Sweet Shoppe

Hand woven tapestry; perle cotton, wool, cow hair; 54 by 49 inches.
Photo: Michael H. Rubin

Based on a black-and-white photo of my husband and his sister in front of their father's New York soda shop. I immediately responded to the grid (checkerboard) behind them. The grid, a recurring theme in my work, symbolizes the game of life and society's constraints.

B

Ruth Scheuer

Narcissus #2 - How Can I Reach That Loveliness?

Tapestry; wool, cotton, plexiglass; 40 by 24 by 10 inches.
Photo: Elijah Cobb

"How Can I Reach That Loveliness?" shows the entrapment of self-involvement. The tapestry is folded, like a mirror, with wings of the image at both ends reflected in repetition. The roots of narcissism are ancient to our culture, yet the image we have reflected back to us is that of ourselves, and others in whom we see ourselves reflected.

B

C

C

Cecilia Blomberg

Papouss II

Flat tapestry, soumak, brocading; cotton twine, wool, linen; 58 by 41 inches.

D

Alison Keenan

Haida at Granville Island

Gobelin tapestry; cotton, wool; 34 by 43 inches.
Photo: Barbara Cohen

E

Barbara Heller

The Last Resort

Tapestry, hand spinning and dyeing; linen, cotton, wool; 60 by 48 inches.

This image was inspired by a series of snapshots taken by my father in 1920. I sought to capture the faded glory of the time, the isolation wealth brings, the refusal to see outside one's reality.

D

E

A

Frances Key

Bathers

Gobelin tapestry; wool, cotton;
72 by 54 inches.

B

Valerija Purlyte

Renaissance

Tapestry; wool, linen; 170 by
200 cm.

C

Tricia Goldberg

Odette

Tapestry; wool, silk, cotton;
46 by 46 inches.
Photo: Bruce Handelsman

D

Inge Norgaard

Heimdals Nine Mothers

Free-style Gobelin tapestry;
linen, wool, vegetal dyes; 54
by 96 inches.
Photo: Charles Haniford

*This is my way of translating
the images from my psyche
into tangible form.*

A

A

Anne G. Clark

I Have No Head

Tapestry; wool, photographic paper; 25 by 34 inches.

Incorporating the photographic image of a garden fountain, this weaving examines the strange perceptions that develop with dementia. The old patterns are still there but the connections memory provides are lost.

B

Marcel Marois

Passage interrompu

High warp tapestry; wool; 106 by 128 inches.
Photo: Yves Martin.

B

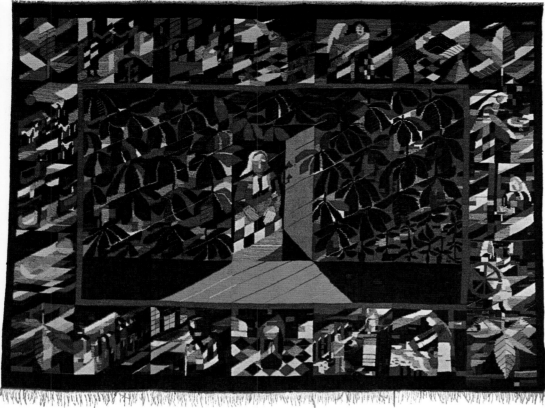

C

Zinaida Jockute-Martinaitiene
Thoughts

Tapestry; wool, linen; 350 by
220 cm.
Photo: Alg. Kezys

*The work is dedicated to dear,
honest country folk. My grand-
mother Barbora stands at her
cottage. She is encircled by
youth, works, a prayer and
a coffin.*

D

I. Wojciech-Jaskolka
Expectation and Fulfillment

Tapestry, vertical warp; wool,
linen, sisal, nylon; 210 by
150 cm.

D

A

Micala Sidore

Blues for Peter Stein

Traditional French woven
tapestry; wool; 41 by 30½ inches.
Photo: Stephen Petegorsky

B

Pamela Topham

Accabonac Harbor Morning

Tapestry, twilling; silk, wool,
cotton; detail, full piece; 34 by
46 inches.
Photo: Rameshwar Das

C

Margo MacDonald

Oprah

Tapestry; cotton, wool; 38½ by
21 inches.

*This is a frozen moment of
reality at home with my small
children. I always fold laundry
while watching Oprah.*

B

C

D

D

Kaija Tyni-Rautiainen
On The West Coast
Tapestry; linen; 75 by 58 inches.
Photo: Barbara Cohen

E

Alexandra Friedman
Adirondack
Modified Gobelin tapestry; wool,
linen; 51 by 66 inches.

E

A

Pat Johns

Blown Tulips, Inca Rug

Flat woven tapestry; wool, silk, linen, cotton; 36 by 38 inches.

B

Whitney Peckman

Calla Lilies

Moorman threading technique; cotton, wool, silk; 48 by 66 inches.

C

Janet Moore

Hekolas

Shaped tapestry; wool, cotton; 40 by 78 inches.

Hekolas is the guardian spirit of my home and perhaps an interior portrait.

A

B

C

D

D

Martha Matthews

Day Lily

Tapestry; wool, linen, cotton;
62 by 42½ inches.

E

Jeni Ross

The Isle is Full of Noises

Gobelin tapestry; wool, linen,
silk, cotton; 1¾ by 1½ m.

The design is inspired by Shakespeare's "Tempest." The central figure, while being based on Caliban, also owes something to the West Indian/African mythical creature Anansi.

E

A

Care Standley

Fragmented

Tapestry; cotton, wool, silk; 16 by 12 inches.
Photo: Kim Harrington

Tapestry is a curiously satisfying form. It's a visual exploration of ideas and obsessions which involves a delicate balance between spontaneous design and exact execution.

B

Helga Berry

Passage thru Time

Tapestry; wool, silk, synthetics; 50 by 38 inches.
Photo: Chris Arend

C

Deborah Hobbins

Magic Carpet #6

Tapestry; linen, wool; 55 by 36 inches.
Photo: Roger LePage

C

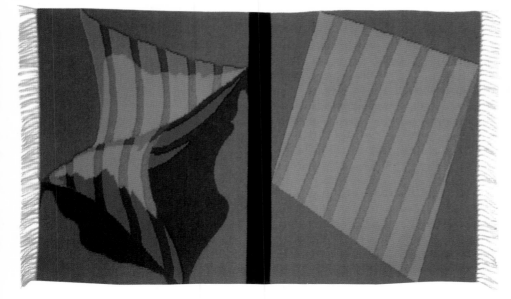

D

Elinor Steele

Techno-Pastorale

Tapestry; wool, cotton; 22 by 48 inches.

This is a visual oxymoron and an abstract self-portrait. I am interested in computer graphics and high-tech images, and yet I choose a low-tech medium for expression.

E

Alina Briedelyte-Kavaliauskiene

The Milky Way

Tapestry; wool, silk, linen; 250 by 250 cm.
Photo: Vytautas Vilaniskis

F

Audrey Moore

Magic from a Red Robe

Woven on Navajo loom; hand-dyed wool; 40 by 40 inches.
Photo: Jerome Hart

D

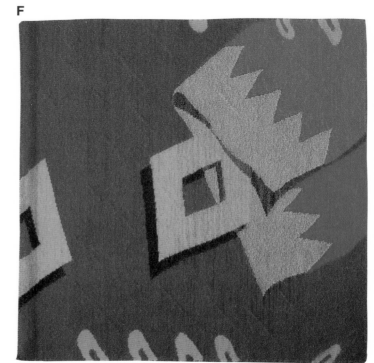

E

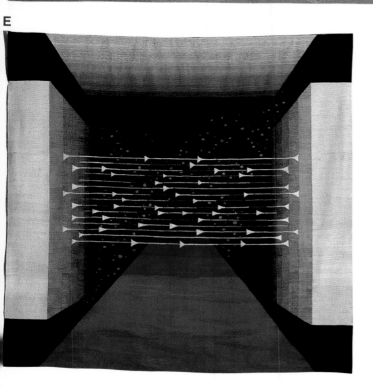

F

A

B

C

A

Ruth Manning

Diner Reflections

Tapestry; cotton seine twine, wool; 39 by 25 inches.
Photo: Kamper Productions, Ltd.

Having always been fascinated with diners, I was drawn to this gem in Rochester, New York. Many cups of coffee later, the design was produced for the piece.

B

Victor Jacoby

Narrow Passage

Tapestry; wool, cotton; 36 by 47 inches.
Photo: James D. Toms

This tapestry is a personal land-scape, a place that I have experienced both physically and emotionally.

C

Rita Romanova Gekht

Constructive Interlude

Tapestry; wool, cotton; 40 by 64 inches.

I find interesting similarities between weaving a tapestry and constructing a building: starting from the bottom, building one shape on top of another, binding them together.

D

Joyce Hulbert

Icon

Tapestry; hand-dyed wool; 66 by 42 inches.

Fiber, and wool in particular, imparts to color the great quality of saturation. By dyeing my yarns, I achieve a personal palette that addresses the content of my imagery and the symbolic character of color.

E

Judith Verostko-Petree

My Mother Had Me In Another World

Tapestry weave; wool, linen; 48 by 72 inches.
Photo: Taylor Dabney

D

E

A

Mary Lane

Rags and Tatters

Gobelin tapestry; cotton, wool, metallics; 34½ by 59½ inches.
Photo: Dennis Griggs

My intention is to involve the viewer, to elicit a reaction beyond the imagery. I want to provoke thought and stimulate an active relation between the viewer and my work.

B

Mary-Ann Sievert

To Vera

Tapestry; wool, cotton; 3½ by 6½ inches.
Photo: Rita Gecht

I deliberately contradict any logical sense of three-dimensional space. As a result, the image refuses to be perceived realistically.

C

Lynn Basa

Yolk Play

Tapestry; silk, wool, cotton, linen; 8 by 8 inches.
Photo: UW-IMA

D

Lore Edzard

Meeting

Gobelin tapestry; wool, cotton; 45 by 64 inches.

I've spent my life in two different worlds: many years in Germany where I was influenced by Expressionism, and in the U.S. intrigued by North American Indian Art.

Somewhere between these two cultures, I try to find myself.

E

Lynn Mayne

Containment

Tapestry; wool, linen; 36 by 28 inches.

F

Bonnie Britton

Double X

Flat weave; handspun wool; 60 by 84 inches.
Photo: John Babcock

A

B

C

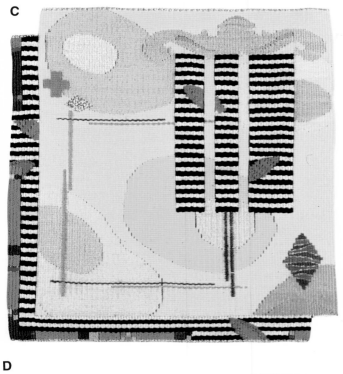

E

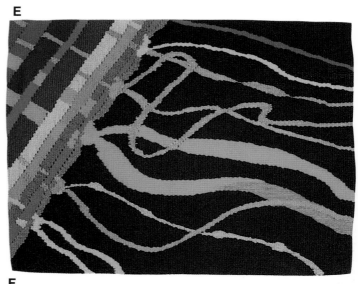

D

F

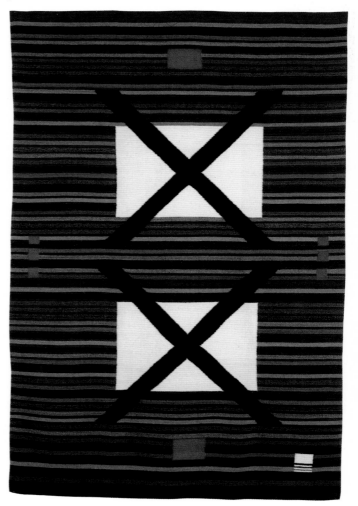

A
Jay Wilson
Colorflight

Plain tapestry; wool, linen, vegetable dye; 79 by 48 inches.
Photo: Paul Kodama, Honolulu

The design is taken directly from a photo of huckleberry bushes which appeared in The Nature Conservancy magazine. My intention was not to make a tapestry which looked like a photograph, but to turn a photo into a weaving.

B
Jitka Stenclova
Paradigm

Tapestry; wool, cotton; 170 by 90 cm.

C
C. Elizabeth Smathers
Autumn's Transitions

Tapestry; wool, mohair, linen; 31 by 24 inches.
Photo: Richard Smathers

Fall is the time of year I love most. It gives me a feeling of calm, yet excites me with renewed energy.

This piece was commissioned for one of the libraries at Vanderbilt University. To me, a library can do the same with the quiet calm, yet the books open new ideas and energy.

A

B

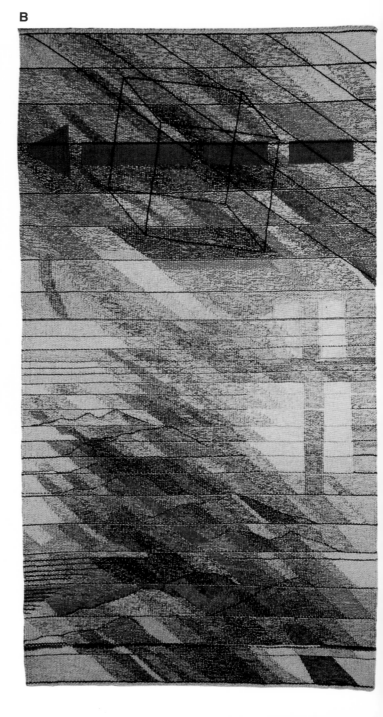

C

D

Philadelphia Fiber Studio

Leaf I

Gobelin tapestry; cotton, wool; 30 by 48 inches.

The artists of PFS work collectively and interchangeably in all stages of a tapestry.

E

Stephen Thurston

Hi Light

Aubusson tapestry; wool, silk, rayon, cotton, metallic threads; 54 by 90 inches.

D

E

A

Sheila Held

Wonderland Through the Looking Glass

Tapestry, interlocked weft; wool, metallics, cotton; 38 by 50 inches.
Photo: Dave Altman

Just as all matter exists in quantified units, so is a tapestry built up fiber by fiber, block by block.

B

Fuyuko Matsubara

The Air in the Soil II

Painted warp, weft, inlay; linen, ramie, cotton; 43 by 34 inches.

A

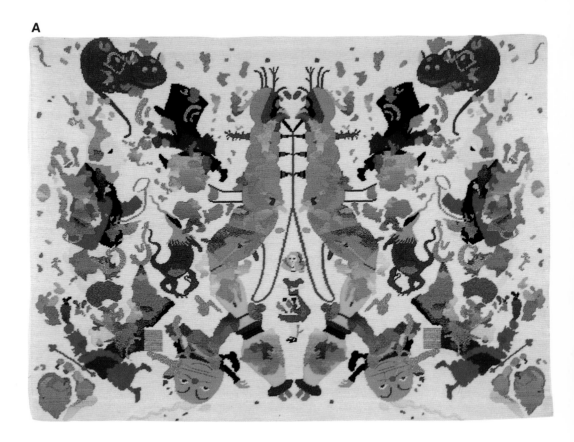

B

C

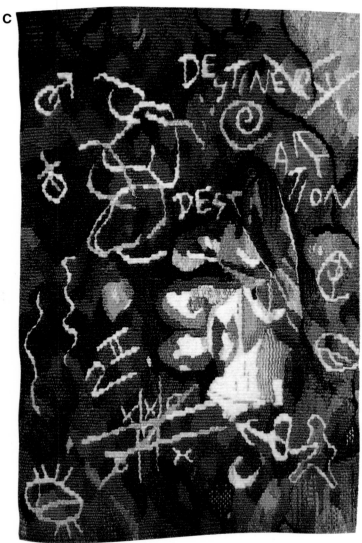

C

Shelley Socolofsky

Still Life With Hieroglyphs & Glove

Flat tapestry; wool, silk; 6 by 12 inches.

I do not wish to deny tapestry's history, but to critically address it, to go beyond the tradition, speak directly to the cloth, redefine what constitutes tapestry in my own terms.

D

David Johnson

Riff In Blue

Tapestry; wool, cotton; 54 by 35 inches.

I weave the movement and interaction of lines freely derived from music. Ideally, one could hear as well as see the tapestry.

D

A

Susan Iverson

Ancient Burial IV - Night

Tapestry; wool, linen; 90 by 72 inches.
Photo: Katherine Wetzel

This tapestry is about pre-Colombian Peruvian textiles, their burial and rediscovery.

B

Kristin Carlsen Rowley

Torn Apart

Tapestry; dyed wool, linen; 120 by 44 inches.

A

B

C

C

Ann Baddeley Keister

Three Rooms, Ocean View

Tapestry; wool, cotton; 43½ by 68 inches.
Photo: David Keister

D

Murray Gibson

Le Jardin des Etoiles

Slit tapestry; wool, silk, metallics, cotton; 55 by 56 inches.

The design was inspired by the Aurora Borealis. All of the star motifs have been drawn from Middle Eastern kilims.

E

Carol Duesbury

Natural Elements

Wool; 54 by 58 inches.

I live on the high mesa of New Mexico and am very influenced by that environment. The random placement of stones, rocks and formations and colors seems so perfect, as if it were laid out to tell the big secret. One thing for sure, though—the universe doesn't speak English.

D

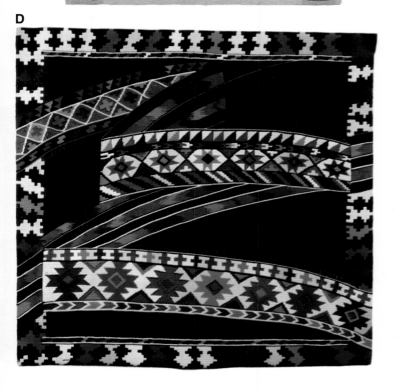

E

A

Dale Jackson

Point of View

Gobelin tapestry; wool, silk, cotton; 60 by 84 inches.
Photo: Rick Chard

This piece is the result of a lichen-covered wall in the Philippines. I wanted the viewer to have the feeling of moving beyond or through the wall.

B

Carol Russell

Fira/Dawn #2

Traditional tapestry: slits, blended and eccentric wefts; cotton, wool, silk; 29 by 24 inches.
Photo: George Mauro

C

Mary Kester

Bright, Lite

Multi-layered, traditional tapestry; wool, cotton; 48 by 42 by 4 inches.

Just as my subject matter has surface detail and substance, I look to form as object and image. With overlapping edges and subtle coloring, I create an illusion of depth.

D

Betty Vera

Byrdcliffe Woods

Painted warp, mixed twills, discontinuous weft inlays, stitching; cotton, linen; 61 by 56 inches.
Photo: Earl Ripling

E

Sharon Marcus

Time Marker

Gobelin tapestry; cotton, wool, goat hair; 59½ by 38¼ inches.
Photo: Bill Bachhuber

I seek a deliberate ambiguity of meaning through greater abstraction of the image.

F

Robin Knight

Reflections

Tapestry weaving, Rio Grande method; wool; 32 by 43 inches.
Photo: Robert Ames Cook

The design depicts the colors and landscapes of northern New Mexico.

A

B

C

D

E

F

A

Inger Lise Rodli

Return of the Sun

Tapestry; wool, linen; 90 by 90 cm.

B

Feliksas Jakubauskas

In Remembrance/White, Signifying

French gobelin tapestry; linen, wool, silk, synthetics; 187 by 312 cm.
Photo: O. Petrauskas

This work was created during a time of political upheaval in Lithuania. It was a time marked by the collapse of a repressive system which deeply affected the work of artists. My tapestry reflects this momentous change.

C

Constance Hunt

Aftershock

Tapestry; wool, cotton; 18 by 12 inches.
Photo: Gary Hunt

My house and studio were in shambles from the October 17, 1989 Bay Area earthquake. I drew and re-drew my broken china, then added the actual seismographic chart.

D

Aleksandra Manczak

Close-up

Gobelin tapestry, double warp; wool, cotton; 225 by 150 cm.

With double warp, I "translate" photos into tapestry. This piece was inspired by the triptych form from Medieval times.

A

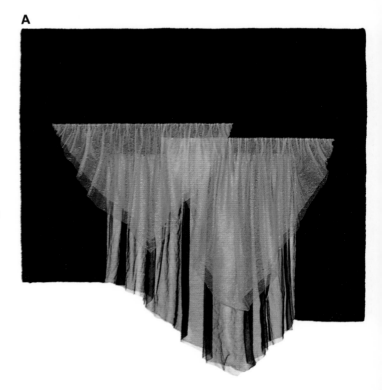

B

C

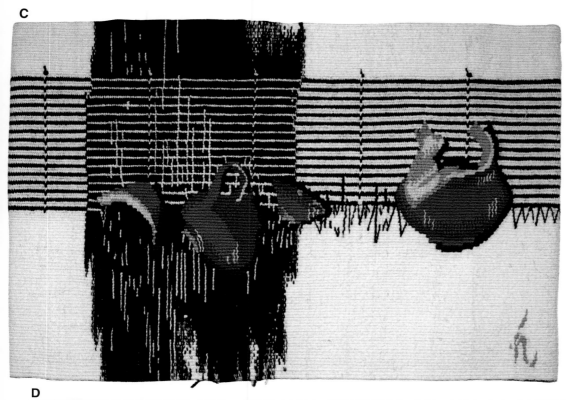

D

A

Margrit Sutter-Furrer
Panta rhei
Gobelin tapestry; wool; 190 by
126 cm.

B

Judith Kohn
Village and Sky
Weft mixing, slit, interlocking
joins; wool, cotton; 38 by 43
inches.
Photo: Preston Kohn

*An architecturally-inspired
tapestry. In the 1970s I lived in
Morocco where intense colors,
inward-looking architecture,
contrasts of shadow and light,
tricks of visual perception are
all commonplace. These have
since become themes in much
of my work.*

C

Betty Vera
That Which Has No Name
Painted warp, mixed twills, 4-
harness weaves, discontinuous
wefts; cotton, linen; 63 by 78
inches.
Photo: Earl Ripling

*The grassy landscape is a visual
metaphor for the intangible,
unnameable life force that per-
meates the natural world.*

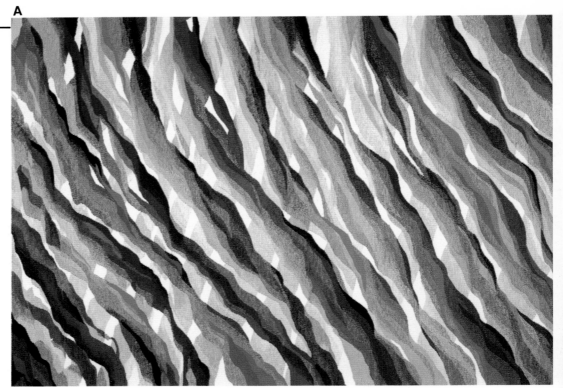

C

D

E

D

Marti Fleischer
Mildred, c. 1920

Needlewoven; cotton, embroidery floss; 3¾ by 5¾ inches.
Photo: University of Tennessee
Art Department

E

Janet Austin
Thin Model

Tapestry; wool, cotton; 11 by
14 inches.

*I found this in an old sketch pad
of mine. When I did the sketch,
I had a hard time with the model
being very thin, until the day she
wore a bathrobe.*

A

Jeyhan Rohani
Ayat Al Kursi

Gobelin tapestry; cotton, wool;
57⅛ by 41⅝ inches.
Photo: Dianne Walker

*I weave Islamic calligraphy and
take my inspiration from the
calligraphers of the past.*
   *This piece took about two
years to develop the calligraphy
and five months to weave.*

B

Ursula Jaeger
Versiegeltes Tor

Gobelin tapestry; cotton, linen;
160 by 160 cm.

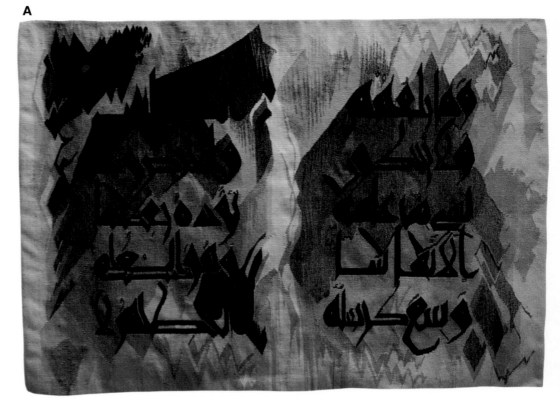

PAPER AND FELT

Leena Ketola-Jokinen
The King of Games
Laminate, painting; handmade
paper, silk, paint; 150 by 250 cm.
Photo: Johnny Korkman

A
Laurel Covington-Vogl

Gift Packages for Toyokuni

Handmade paper, origami; abaca, marbled paper; 24 by 30 inches.

B
Karen McCarthy

Black Pool Fragment

Plaiting, drawing, painting, stitching; paper, paint, pastels, rice paste; 18 by 18 inches.

I worked this construction in layers. Metallic paint is adhered to woven paper which is later stitched, drawn into and constructed. These methods allow me to re-work to achieve surfaces of depth and variation.

A

B

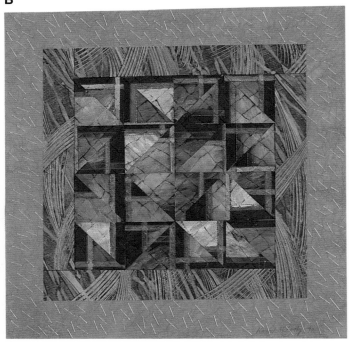

C

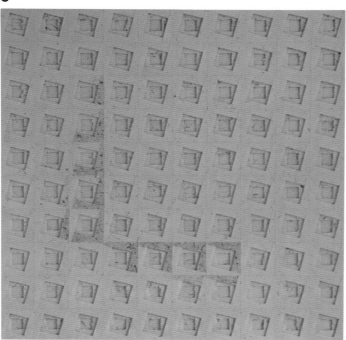

D

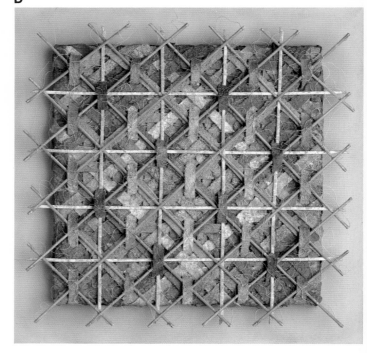

44

C

Ursula Buller
Untitled
Tearing, glueing; handmade paper, plants, cardboard; 120 by 120 cm.

D

Barbara Allen
Stick Construction Number 4
Woven off the loom, spraying; hand blown paper, linen, sticks, pastels, pigments; 28 by 28 by 2 inches.
Photo: Thomas Mezzanotte

The paper was made by hanging a bed sheet on a clothes line and spraying the pulp from a popcorn gun. Whenever I do the process, I invite friends to join me. Our efforts produce some of the most glorious "laundry" in the state of Connecticut.

E

Roberta Fountain
Teapots In Space
Poured handmade paper, embellished, embroidered; paper, fabric, sequins, acrylics, ink; 29½ by 22 inches.

F

Lynn Sures
Lucy
Handmade paper; cotton, abaca, flax, pigment; 43 by 75 inches.

Tribute to ancient Hominid skeleton, a female ancestor of the current human race, found in Africa.

G

Chad Alice Hagen
Rugs From Mars: Deconstruction of Radishes
Felting; wool; 99 by 86 inches.

E

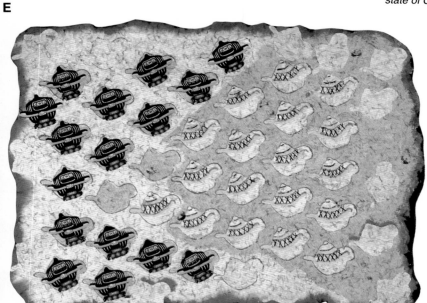

F

G

E

F

Jonna Gibson
Tiles On Tides #1

Handmade felt, raku; wool, ceramics; 17½ by 18 inches.

I enjoy the challenge of combining and manipulating seemingly unlike materials and processes.

B

Pat Gentenaar-Torley
Nick of Time

Handmade paper; silk, cotton, flax, linen, abaca, straw, sisal, kozo; 90 by 140 cm.

I work in a meditative manner. My visual language is pulled from my unconscious and I express in my work what I cannot express with words.

C

Susan Warner Keene
Transformations of Regret: Version 1

Papermaking, felting; flax, cotton, dye, acrylic paint; 26 by 36 by 3 inches.

Textiles mediate between nature and human culture, belonging to both yet to neither. My work attempts to chart some of this ambiguous territory where we face the dilemma of our implication in both histories. As objects, these pieces are equally artifacts of need and speculation.

D

Maria Stachowska
Lights & Shadows

Dyeing, feltmaking; wool, silk; 73 by 118 cm.
Photo: Edward Brandon

E

Karen Page
Cryptic Configuration #4

Felting; wool; 106 by 80 inches.

The conscious decision to work in the medium of felt for non-functional pieces is a declaration against the homogeneity of the mass-produced.

F

Elizabeth Holster
Aerial Carrots

Collage, drawing, painting; handmade paper; 42 by 18 inches.

Imagine helicopters shaped like carrots, whirling madly through space!

A

Cecilia Voss Eager

Pierced Papers #2

Painting, plaiting; cotton rag paper, reactive dyes; 43 by 40 inches.

I'm exploring a variety of resist-dye processes. Stencil painting allows me to be spontaneous in my dyework.

B

Carolyn Golberg

Future Past

Handmade paper, watercolor, airbrush, collage; silk, linen, abaca, cotton; 32 by 46 by 2 inches.
Photo: Christine Benkert

I was a garment weaver for 15 years.

C

Norma Langrish

Outburst

Cast paper, shibori silk; cotton, silk, metallics, gold foil, Procion dye; 18 by 26 by 3 inches.
Photo: Barbara Cohen

D

E

F

D

Jane Dunnewold

Tea Party

Handmade paper, stitched, stamped, gold leafed; color Xerox, gold leaf, paint; 9 by 9 by 2 inches.

The entire text is: "I had a little tea party this afternoon at three. 'Twas very small, three guests in all, just I, myself and me. Myself ate up the sandwiches, while I drank up the tea. 'Twas also I who ate the pie and passed the cake to me."

E

Betty Loeffler

Rag Paper

Screened, pressed paper; abaca, kozo, powdered pigments; 4¾ by 8¾ inches. Photo: Lee Dawson

F

Shirley Roese Bahnsen

Firecracker

Plaiting; handmade paper, acrylic paint; 20 by 12 by 6 inches.

A

B

C

D

E

A

Carol McComb

The Clan

Molded paper; cotton linters, waxed string, foil, raffia, sand, embroidery thread; 9 by 18 inches.
Photo: Scotty McComb

As a result of a trip through the Southwest, I became intrigued with the culture of the Anasazi Indians. How they survived a harsh and demanding land with beauty and grace haunts my imagination.

B

Jane Case Vickers

Pierced

Forming; handmade paper, pastels, enamel; 96 by 48 by 12 inches.
Photo: A. E. Davis

C

Theresa Morin

Wheel

Cast paper; cotton rag, methyl cellulose; 24 by 30 inches each.

D

Karen White

Granite Series III

Dyed and formed paper pulp; handmade paper, dye, styrofoam, wood; 26 by 18 by 8 inches.
Photo: Boyd B. Burkhart

E

Liz Curtin

Dreams of Summer Gardens

Collage; cast paper, Xeroxed fabric; 18½ by 16½ by 2 inches.
Photo: D. James Dee.

B

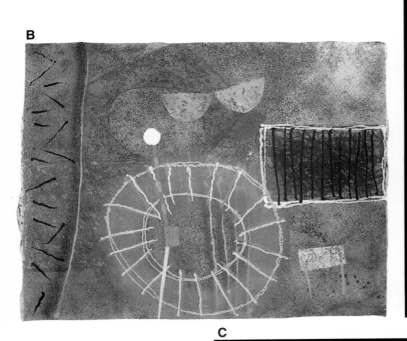

C

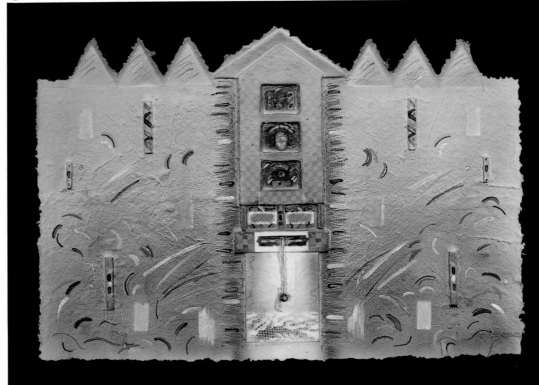

D

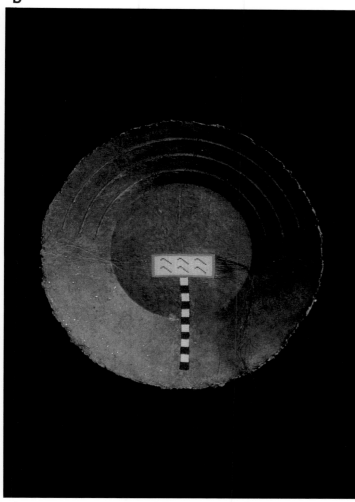

A

Tracy Krumm
Undergoing Transformations

Weaving, mixed media; abaca, cotton, oatmeal paper, rayon, acrylics, oil and chalk pastels, prismacolor; 48 by 58 inches. Photo: Jay Graham

My work has evolved into a series of "pages" that tell a story about me. How I relate to others and to my surroundings are recurring images.

B

Richard Hungerford
Walking Stick Dreamtime

Painting; pigmented paper pulp; 72 by 96 inches. Photo: Dennis Sullivan

C

Mona Waterhouse
Spirit House: Secret Places

Sheet-formed paper, airbrushed; cotton pulp, dye, paint, pastels; 37 by 26 inches.

Often there is an opening in my work, where mysterious objects and landscapes exist. My intent is to reveal the extraordinary that lies just below the surface.

D

Susan Planalp
Pathway Bowl

Handcast paper, loomed bead-work; handmade paper, beads; 16 by 16 by 3½ inches. Photo: Todd Misk

My imagery and color comes from studying Amish quilt colors and basket patterns from Northwest Indian tribes.

E

Genie Shenk
Spiral Ring

Folded paper; armature plex; 132 by 20 by 132 inches. Photo: Susan Einstein

This work explores spiral movement between concentric circles as a metaphor for individual growth, an idea suggested by Navajo, Tantric and Jungian thought.

E

A

A

Deborah Harrington

House Series 2

Feltmaking; felted wool; 24
by 31 inches.
Photo: Red Elf, St. Louis,
Missouri

B

B

Constance Miller

Trellis Recollections

Handmade paper; cotton, dye;
47 by 54 inches.
Photo: Red Elf, St. Louis

C

Lesley Richmond

Denial

Paper casting, collage, dyeing;
silk organdie, abaca paper,
cotton mesh, nails, copper,
computer chips, dye, metallics;
20 by 22 by 2 inches.
Photo: Barbara Cohen

*I've been using the many
textural possibilities of fiber to
create surfaces which suggest
decayed power and faded glory.*

C

D

Sharon Phipps Kump

After the Fall: Experience

Handmade paper, embossing, dyeing; paper, fabric, pastels, dyes, rickrack; 42 by 28 inches.

E

E

Kara Young

Sacred Portal #4

Assemblage, pouring, plastering, staining; abaca, wood, copper, gold leaf, acrylic paint; 18 by 24 inches.
Photo: Roger Nelson

F

Claudia Lee

The Secret Garden

Hand manipulated paper pulp, surface design; cotton linters, dyes, ink; 25½ by 15 inches.
Photo: Joe Muncey

The amazing versatility and immediacy of hand papermaking make it an irresistible medium.

Tactily as well as visually it provides the appropriate vocabulary that I require as well as satisfying my need for color and texture while allowing enormous space for creative freedom.

A

Vivian Mak

It's Not My Fault!

Handmade paper; cotton rag;
108 by 26 inches.
Photo: Leo Kwan

The work is based on common responses in conversation. Both English and Chinese are used, but the former is a much smaller size and given subtler treatment so that the viewer must go through the process of discovery. This way, there will be understanding of the meaning of the Chinese words.

B

Molly Fowler

The Dale Family in Vermont

Spinning, felting, knotless netting; wool, silk, ramie, wire, resin; 38 by 67 by 7 inches.

The Dale family collects maple sap to take to the sugar house. In late winter the pond is still frozen, cows graze on winter stubble, and the ski slopes are silhouetted against an evening sky.

C

Marjorie Tomchuk

Red Planet

Embossing, dyeing; handmade paper, dye; 25 by 36 inches.

Carol McKie Manning and Christen Brown

Medicine Woman/Snake Charmer

Appliqué, quilting, trapunto, embroidery; nylon, rayon, lamé, metallics, beads; 66 by 36½ inches.
Photo: Tom Henderson

This ensemble was inspired by a trip to Santa Fe and a primitive art show at the De Young Museum in San Francisco.

A

B

C

D

E

F

A

Debra Maringo-Meteney

Purple Dunes

Woven and warp painted on the loom; cotton, silk, cotton/linen, fiber reactive dyes.
Photo: Tony Kambic

B

Beverly Ryan

Black & White & Red All Over

Woven, embellishment; silk, rayon, cotton, ribbon, buttons.
Photo: Richard Rodriquez

Bold, geometrical shapes catch my eye and imagination. It's fascinating to create them in textiles and to wear them with a wink and a smile.

C

Marguerite Schreiber

Autumn and Spring #2

Handwoven; rayon, cotton.
Photo: George Anderson

D

Jo Hill

Woven Jacket

Weaving, crochet; wool, mohair.
Photo: J. Daniels

E

Katherine Sylvan

Rubies: Jewel Series

Weaving; dyed silk.
Photo: Valerie Santagto

F

Cathy Peckens

Rainbow Spectrum Jacket

Handwoven, hairline twill; wool.
Photo: Harriet Wise

A

B

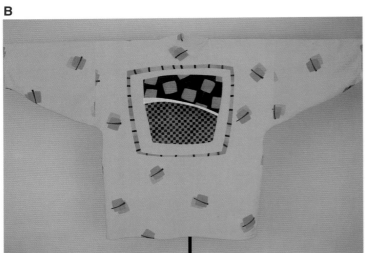

C

D

A

Sanny Nijkamp

Landscape

Gutta resist, machine quilting, painting; silk.

B

Beth Nash

Hand Drum Series - Turquoise

Vat dye, airbrush; raw silk, Procion dye, Dekaperm fabric paint.
Photo: Jerry Anthony

I work with a bold pattern with a scatter pattern around it— chaotic yet orderly.

C

Luanne Rimel

Lava Lights

Painting, dyeing; silk charmeuse, Procion dyes.
Photo: Matt O'Shea

My work is designed to transform a person into a work of art. The images need the movement of a body to be truly appreciated.

D

Jill Branham East

Kandinsky's Coat

Painting; cotton, fiber paint.
Photo: Micah Donovan

In order to get in the mood to do this coat, I played Stravinsky's "The Rites of Spring"—it helped!

E

Susan Holmes

Spinnaker Cloth Raincoat

Appliqué, stencilling; spinnaker cloth.
Photo: Phil Fogle

Even though spinnaker cloth is normally used for making sails, I decided, why not a raincoat?

F

Amy Reich

Nous Allons Au Zoo

Silkscreen, painting; silk, dye, pigment.

I get a lot of inspiration from the world of children. Currently I am working on a hand-painted children's book and on designs for fabric for children's clothes.

E

F

A

B

C

A

Natacha Wolters

Collier ete

Knitting, beading; glass beads, silk thread; 26½ by 23 cm.

I design on a paper grid, where each square is a bead. This collar is made of 38,000 seed beads, but weighs only 105 grams.

B

Susan Penner

Bobbin in Necklace #1

Milanese bobbin lace; silk threads, mahogany bobbin; 12 by 8 inches.
Photo: Jeff Slack

Largely self taught, I take my inspiration from traditional laces, but I feel free enough to use non-traditional applications.

C

Adriane Nicolaisen

Handwoven Ruana

Woven; mohair, wool, cotton, rayon; 48 by 72 inches.
Photo: Jess Shirley

D

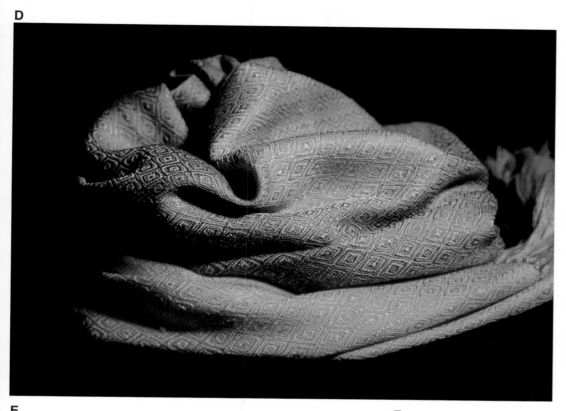

D

Renata Brink

Untitled

Ikat, dyeing; silk; 20 by
50 inches.
Photo: Kai Wessel

E

Mary Bentley

Fire and Ice

Summer and winter weave, inlay;
hand-dyed silk; 12 by 62 inches.
Photo: Barbara Cohen

F

Elizabeth Bell

Goldfish Scarf

Woven, painted warp; silk; 12½
by 60 inches.
Photo: Barbara Cohen

*The color scheme and design
were inspired by Matisse's
painting, "The Goldfish Bowl."
By painting the warp I can have
a changing background and a
greater color range.*

*I particularly enjoy the free-
dom of applying the dye to the
warp threads.*

E

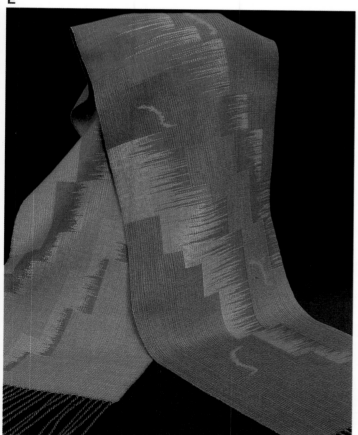

F

A

Diane Easton

Untitled Kimono

Dyeing; cotton, rayon; 62 by
49 inches.

B

Nancy Kotch-Howell

Tulip Kimono

Tapestry; wool, linen, silk.

C

Bonnie Benson

Rhapsody in Blue

Piecing, quilting; cotton.
Photo: M. Koen

*The Royal Palace in Bangkok
was the inspiration for this piece.*

D

Dagmar Klos

Silk Kimono

Handwoven, 8 harness huck;
silk.
Photo: Brigid Finucane

*My intent is to produce work that
is both beautiful and functional.*

E

Margrit Schmidtke

Amish Shadowlands I

Quilting, appliqué, painting;
hand-dyed and commercial
cotton; 64 by 54 inches.
Photo: Jonathan Charles

A

B

C

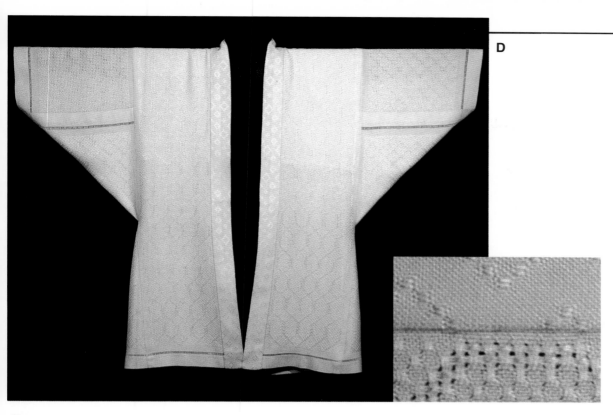

D

E

A

B

C

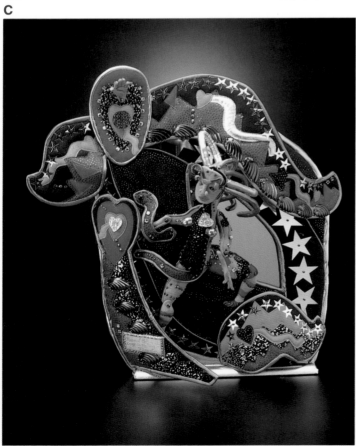

D

E

F

A

Carol Kropnick

Picesaurus

Sewing, quilting, painting; leather; chamois, paint, feathers, beads, velvet; 11 by 11 by 12 inches.
Photo: Maje Waldo

The mask gives us the license to act out, transform, even deceive. It taps into our imagination, emotions and, most of all, our need to transcend our conscious limitations.

B

R. Renee Sherrer

Pasta Dress

Sewing, painting, dyeing; silk organza, pasta, paint, fishing line, kit string, beads.

This dress was made as a challenge to make a garment which was inherently Italian. I like the way it looks like an elegant evening piece from the '20s, but upon closer scrutiny, one learns its secret.

C

Pamela Hastings

Lucy in the Sky

Appliqué, quilting, embellishment; lamé, suede, felt, beads, sequins, buttons; 15 by 15 by 3 inches.
Photo: Allen Bryan

D

Julia Blackwood

General Maintenance

Dyed fabrics, appliqué, quilting; cotton, leather, suede, silk, bulbs, found objects.
Photo: Fabrice Ternois

This piece is part of a series which takes a whimsical look at various occupations. Social commentary is quilted into the spaces around the objects.

E

Suzanne Bracker

Untitled #2

Machine knitting, crochet; cotton, linen, rayon, silk, wool.
Photo: Len Kawecki

F

Wendy Ross

Woodland Faerie

Gutta resist, painting, appliqué, beading; silk, dried flowers and moss, beads, sequins.
Photo: Linda Sweeting

A

Margaret Roach Wheeler

Desert Memories

Handwoven, felted; wool, cotton.
Photo: Gayden Shell

B

Giselle Shepatin

Untitled

Weaving; silk, cotton, rayon,
ramie, nylon.
Photo: Tia Dodge

C

Giselle Shepatin

Untitled

Sewing; silk, cotton, rayon;
necklace by Susan Green.
Photo: Tia Dodge

D

Seong Hee Kim

Sun

Hand knitting; wool, cotton.
Photo: Chong Eik Park

*My main interest was in working
on the color gradation.*

E

**Joan Hall-Jones and Philippa
Drummond**

Evening Velvet

Rosepath woven; wool, chenille.

F

Pia Filliger-Nolte

Variation of Three Squares

Plain weave; silk, wool.
Photo: Rosi Radecke

A

B

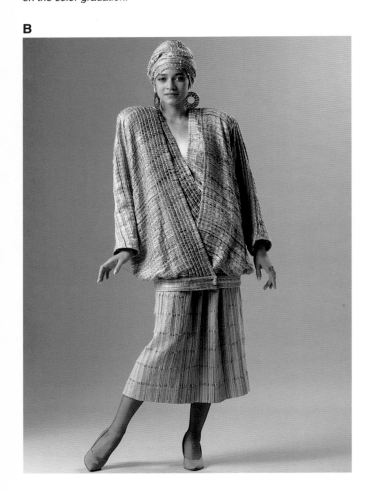

C

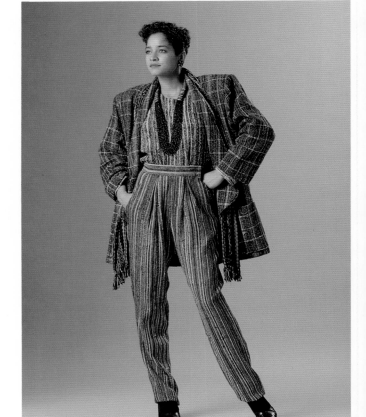

D

F

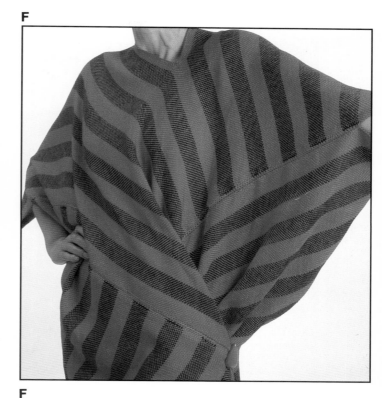

E

F

A

Alicia Niles

Untitled Coat

Machine knitting; wool, cotton, rayon, lurex, polyester, mohair.

I was inspired by the rich jewel tones of the golds, rusts and lapis lazuli colors from King Tutankhamun's reign. When I saw the Tutankhamun sarcophagus, I felt a royal, untouchable presence, a lasting power. With this coat I wanted to maintain that attitude.

B

Robin Bergman

Harlequin Clouds

Hand loomed, knitted; silk, rayon.
Photo: Thayer Morgan

C

Robin Bergman

Boiled Wool Coat

Knitted; 100% wool, ultrasuede trim.
Photo: Thayer Morgan

To create the boiled wool, original patterns are knit into loose yardage, which is then shrunk into a dense yet flexible fulled fabric through abrasion and washing with hot and cold water. The fulled yardage is blocked, cut and sewn into a finished garment.

D

Allison Doherty and Karen Overtoom/Animalistic Outerwear

Felt Coat, Hat, Bag

Feltmaking; felted wool.

Each of our pieces is a marriage of our different tastes and influences.

E

Erika Baker

Southwest Coat

Machine knitting; wool, silk, angora mohair.
Photo: Joseph Giunta

A

B

C

D

E

A

Mary Preston

Creation Coat - Raven: Mysteries Part I

Stencilling, painting, embroidery; linen, cotton, fabric paint, ribbons, beads.

I love reading the mythology of the coastal and Alaskan peoples. A few years ago I was drawn to the stories about Raven, the trickster god. I feel a very deep connection with animals and discovered that Raven is reputed to watch over the spirits of all animals.

B

Jewell Peterson

Bolero

Dyeing, crochet, sewing, machine embroidery; felted wool, English mohair.

The process by which wool fibers form into felt fabric has fascinated me for 20 years. I used to sculpt clay, but gave it up when I learned to "sculpt" fiber into wearables.

As I design each new piece, I imagine where on the body each dab of color will go.

A

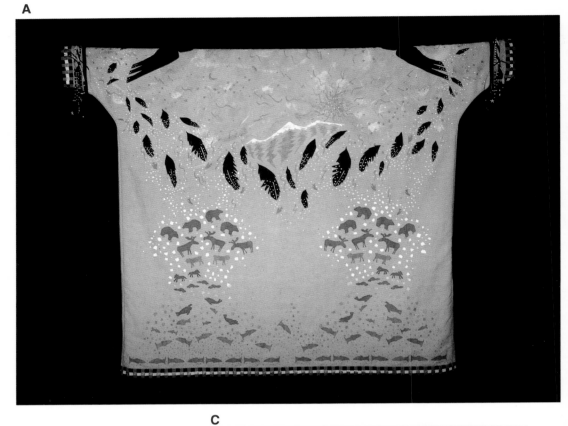

B

C

72

D

E

F

A

Peggy Loughlin DeBell

Pompeii Fish

Printing, painting; cotton, cast paper, pearl paints, glitter.
Photo: Al Nuckols

The fish images are rubbings from a fish which was kept in the freezer for eight months; it was used over and over for other projects.

B

Michelle Marcuse

Painted Silk Outfit

Direct dye application; silk shantung, crepe de chine, wax resist.
Photo: Lindy Powers

C

Jytte Rasmussen

Untitled

Dyeing, silk.
Photo: Jens Petersen

QUILTING

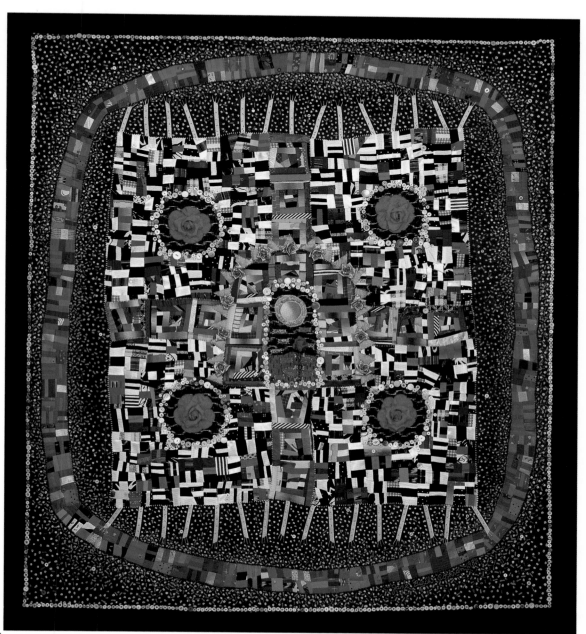

Jane Burch Cochran
Ring Around the Roses, Ring Around the Moon

Machine pieced, appliqué, painted; commercial fabric, buttons, beads, paint, artificial flowers; 68 by 77 inches. Photo: Pam Monfort

I sketched the idea for this quilt on the plane returning to Kentucky from New Mexico. The colored squares are based on the log cabin pattern but the strips are irregular.

They were fun to piece, like doing small abstract paintings.

A

Sue Benner

Three Times of Sky

Batik, shibori, piecing, machine quilting; silk, cotton; 94 by 54 inches.

Maps, plate tectonics, weather, time, and other physical forces are influences in this work.

B

Nancy Erickson

Vesuvius Revisited: Model and Capybaras

Machine appliqué, photographed, quilted; velvet, satin, cotton, paint; 97 by 91 inches.

The lovely model is, alas, unaware of the incipient eruption—and more interested in striking this pose.

C

Janet Page-Kessler

Day Lilies

Machine appliqué, quilting, embroidery; cotton, cotton blends; 36 by 65 inches.

While drawing flowers, I find myself in a trance-like state of concentration. The intricacy and beauty of the shapes and the incredible range of colors add to this state.

Georgia O'Keefe echoed my own feelings: "Whether the flower or the color is the focus, I do not know. I do know the flower is painted large to convey my experience with the flower—and what is my experience if it is not the color?"

D

Marion Ongerth

Shading the Count

Machine piecing and quilting; cotton, cotton blends; 77 by 50 inches.
Photo: Sharon Risedorph

E

Donna Stader

Hem of the Rainbow

Piecing, quilting, appliqué, piping; cotton, cotton blends; 80 by 41 inches.

A

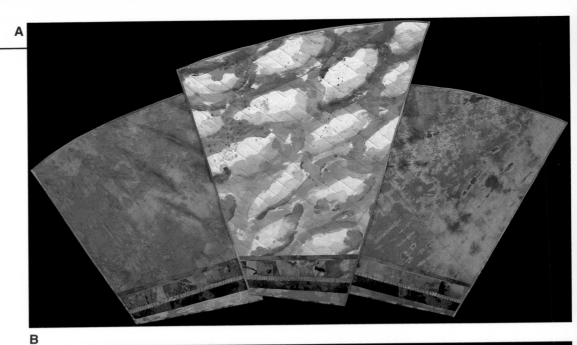

B

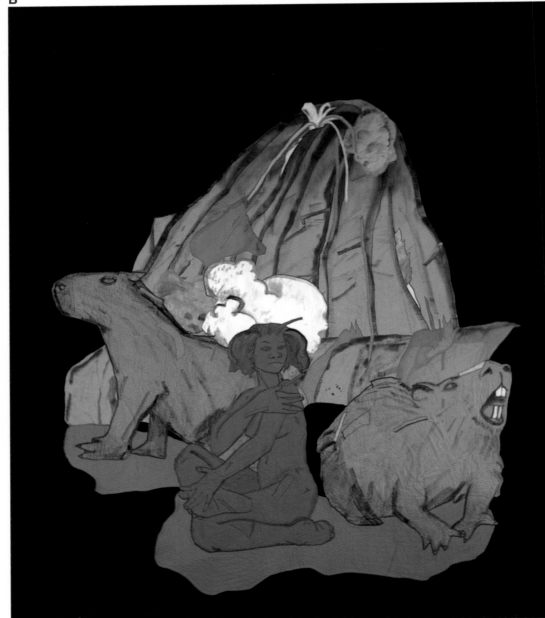

C

D

E

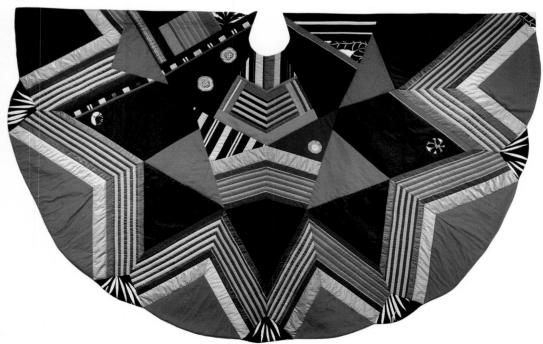

A
Linda Kimura Rees
Fish Bowl

Machine pieced and quilted,
painted and printed fabric;
cotton, fabric paints; 54 by
36 inches.

*My images usually relate to my
cultural heritage in some way.*

B
Marianne McCann Horner
*Backyard-Waterpump-Rocket
Ship*

Stitching; bed sheet, onion bags,
bias tape; 82 by 82 inches.

A

B

C

Carol Adleman

With Picket Fence

Bumaki, cyanotype, hand quilting; cotton; 61 by 76 inches.
Photo: Michael Keefe

The prints have been produced by draping and pleating the fabrics before printing in the sun.

D

Gabrielle Swain

Primary II: Without Provocation

Piecing, appliqué, quilting, slashing; commercial and dyed cotton; 53 by 60 inches.
Photo: Michael Casey

C

D

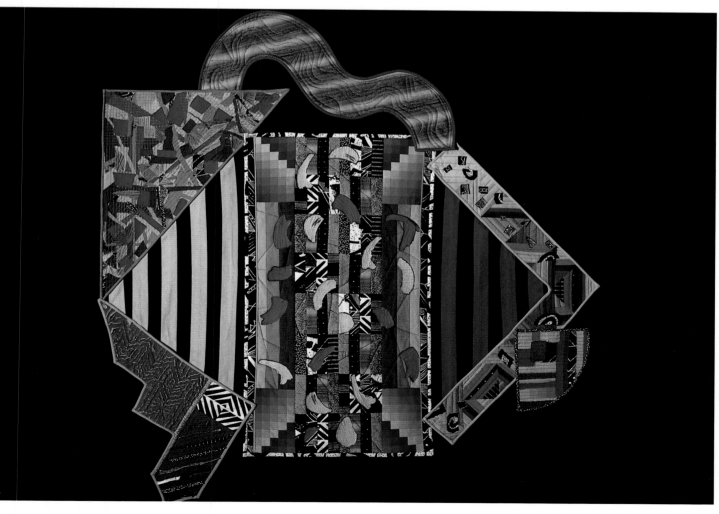

A

Carol Gersen

Squares and Bars

Machine piecing, hand and
machine quilting; cotton,
Procion dyes; 77 by 52 inches.
Photo: Joel Breger

*I began this quilt during the last
weeks of the 1988 presidential
campaign and finished it in
February, 1989—before the
Supreme Court decision on flag
desecration.*

B

Tammy Lavanty

About Face

Hand and machine quilting;
batiked fabric, silk, paint, beads,
floss; 38 by 40 inches.
Photo: Tom Griffen

*This is an exploration of the face
and all of its possibilities.*

C

Dorcas Kraybill

Scissors

Quilting, knotting; cotton, dye,
pastels; 23 by 23 inches.
Photo: Howard Ehrenfeld

*"Scissors" is part of a series
of inanimate objects that are
given a larger-than-life aura
and endowed with a sense of
energy and humor.*

D

Charlotte Butehorn Gabriele

*My Zebra Bleeds Because of
What We've Done*

Hand painting, machine quilting;
unbleached muslin, acrylic paint;
42½ by 54½ inches.

*This quilt was designed to pro-
test the unquestioned applause
that greets many new products
or advancements in civilization
that are made to "make our lives
easier." I wanted to look at some
of these and decide again if
convenience or tradition is
enough of a reason to allow
business and industry to dictate
what is acceptable abuse of the
planet we live on.*

*Some of the "important dates
in history" I chose to show on the
quilt: 1909 - First commercial
manufacture of bakelite marks
beginning of plastic age; 1878 -
Fur farming begins in Canada;
1927 - Airplanes first used to
dust crops with insecticide.*

A

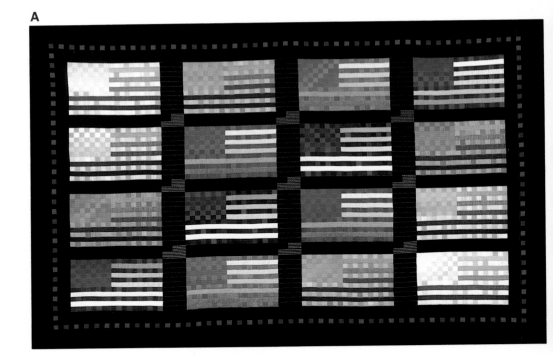

B

E

Marjorie Claybrook

Star Map

Airbrush, appliqué, embroidery, quilting; linen, chintz, broadcloth, sequins, leather, cotton; 37 by 37 inches.
Photo: J. R. Claybrook

F

Gerry Chase

Ordinary Mystics

Machine piecing, hand appliqué and quilting; cotton, ink, crayon, fabric paints; 35 by 32 inches.

My major technical challenge in this quilt was to incorporate line drawings in such a way as to make them feel integral to the overall composition. I felt this called for a collage-like-approach; hence, hand appliqué as the principle method of construction.

The listening attitudes of the figures in this piece remind me of how appealing a contemplative life seems in today's hectic world.

C

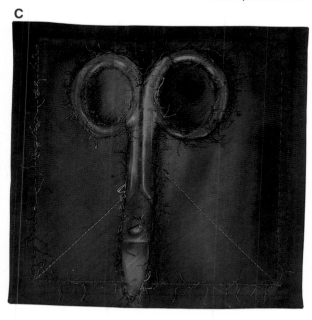

E

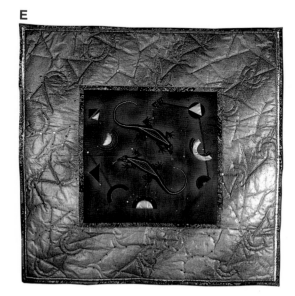

D

F

A
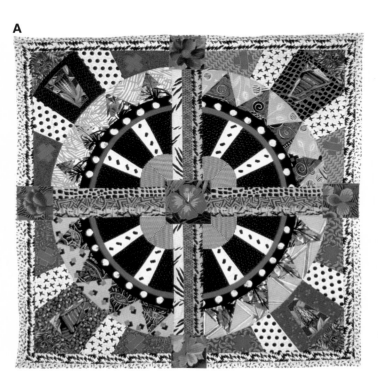

B
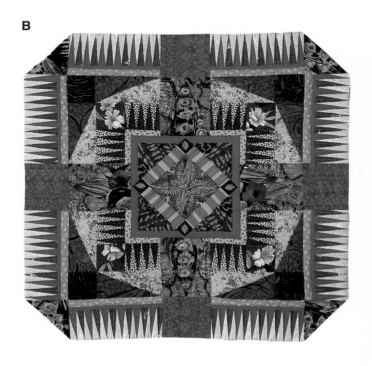

C
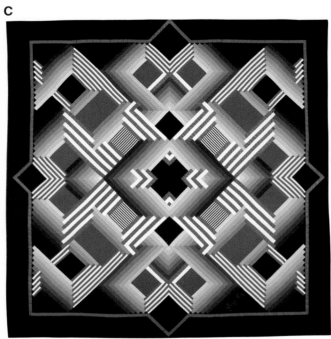

D
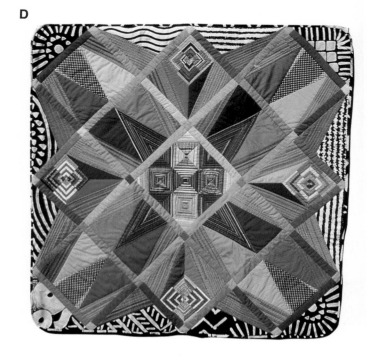

E

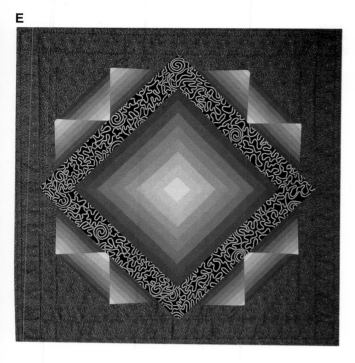

F

A

Jean Neblett

4x4x4: Dance With Life

Machine piecing, appliqué, quilting; cotton, cotton blends; 68 by 68 inches.
Photo: George Post

Color is the most important element in my work. The quilting is free-form and often takes the shape of symbols.

As a former dancer, my work is also about movement: A fast and lively shifting of the eye and senses through color and shape arrangement. This process is very gratifying. Some pieces are sophisticated and elegant, others are elaborate, textural and fun.

B

Gretchen Echols

Garden of Psyche & Amor

Machine pieced, hand quilted; commercial fabrics; 38 by 38 inches.

It is constructed from the center outwards. As I worked creating shapes and choosing colors, I realized that certain areas might not sew together as I planned. The narrow lines of color were devised to fill in the gaps and add elements of strong contrast.

C

Glenda King

LCC 2:3: Structural Conundrum

Machine piecing, hand quilting; cotton, cotton blends; 58 by 58 inches.
Photo: Impact Photography

My interests lie in the exploration of variations possible with log cabin construction.

D

Jan Maher

Thunderbird Tracks III: Reeling

Piecing, quilting; cotton, cotton blends, fabric markers; 38 by 38 inches.

E

Suzanne Evenson

Journey To The Center

Piecing, quilting; commercial and dyed fabric; 35½ by 35½ inches.

This quilt represents the recognition that, despite the many uncertainties in an artist's life, the center is filled with light.

F

Deborah Ellen Davies

Cold Fusion

Piecing, quilting; cotton, linen, rayon; 75 by 75 inches.

The quilt was conceived and constructed during the recent scientific controversy regarding molecular cold fusion. While the "jury" remains divided on the merits of their version, I like to think that mine concludes nicely.

An antique cobweb quilt served as my point of departure for this design. The medallion is my instinct; I rely on the constant equilibrium which it provides. My fascination with this variant of the medallion emerges from the fact that so many straight lines can mimic these graceful circles.

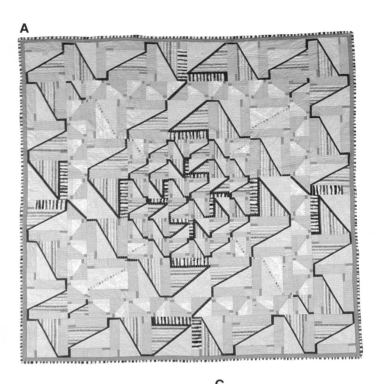

A

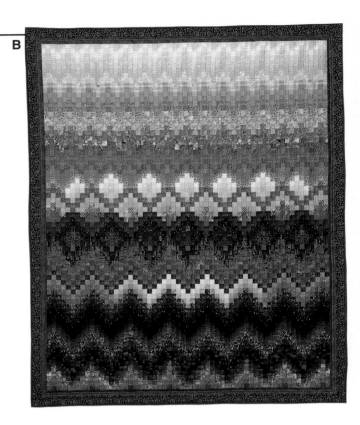

B

C

A

Judy Becker

Response to Granada

Hand quilting, machine piecing;
cotton; 64 by 64 inches.
Photo: David Caras

*In the fall of 1989 I spent time
in Spain. This quilt reflects my
response to the bleached-out
colors of the landscape and
the Moorish architecture of
the Alhambra.*

B

Susan Sawyer

Cedar Winter

Piecing, quilting; cotton; 35
by 43 inches.
Photo: Len Mastri

C

Annette Francoise

Stepping Out

Machine stitched and quilted;
felt, linen, satin, silk; 72 by
74 inches.

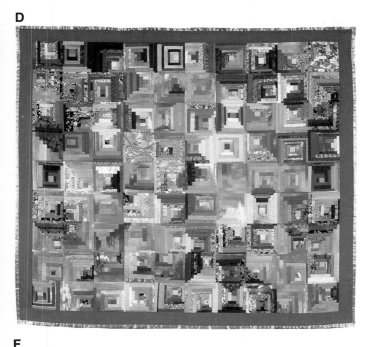

D

E

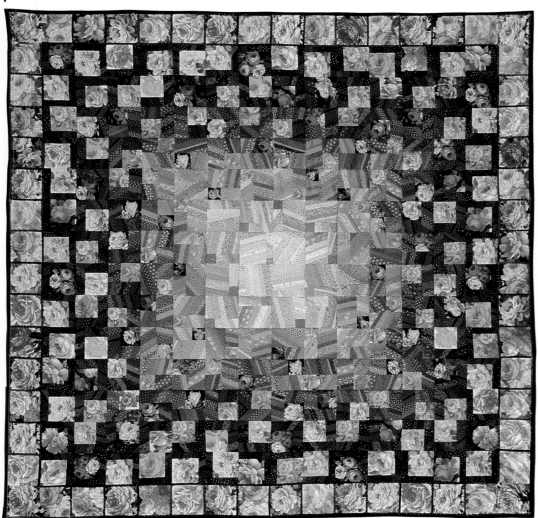

F

D

A. de la Mauviniere Silva

Summer

Machine pieced, hand quilted;
cotton, silk; 62 by 60 inches.
Photo: Michael Bowie

E

Dorle Stern-Straeter

Letter to Milano

Crazy patchwork, machine
piecing, hand quilting; silk,
cotton; 1.55 by 1.10 m.
Photo: Patricia Partl

F

Rachel Liberman

Rose Garden

Machine piecing and quilting;
cotton, cotton blends; 81 by
81 inches.
Photo: David Caras

*This hanging was made in the
spring after I had fallen in love.*

A

Wendy Huhn

Trick-Or-Treat

Hand quilted, machine pieced, painted; cotton, poly/cotton, solvent transfers, fabric paints, charms; 30 by 22 inches.

When placed under a black light, this quilt glows in the dark.

B

Susan Shie and James Acord

The Earth Quilt; a GREEN QUILT

Hand sewn, leather tooled, hand painted; paint, fabric, leather, crystals; 91 by 83 inches. Photo: Visual Impressions

Earth symbolizes many things: survival, groundedness, nurturance, peacefulness, etc. It also obviously has its literal symbol, our planet. In the middle of the over-four-month making of this quilt, we had Earth Day, the 20th anniversary, and also Kent State's 20-year memorial to those who died in war protest.

With this piece, we send out healing energy to earth, the literal ground and rocks and all land creatures; and secondly, to all creatures of all the kingdoms of the other elements—for all need to be balanced if any of us are to survive.

A
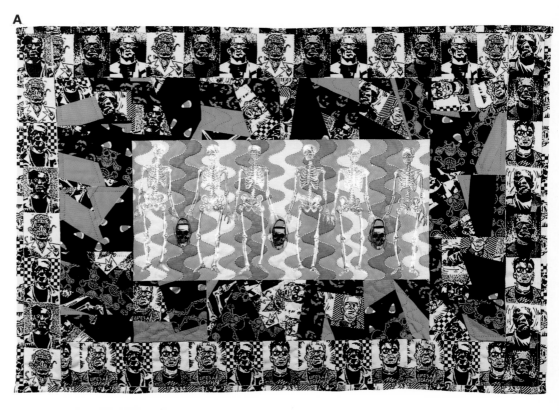

B
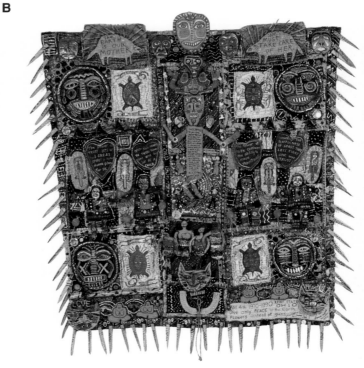

C

Nancy Crasco
Katsuji Wakisaka

Machine pieced, painted, hand quilted; cotton, cotton blends, Deka paints; 54 by 39 inches.
Photo: David Caras

The exotic landscape of Katsuji Wakisaka is part of a series of experiments with painting on quilt tops.

I drew the landscape after the forms were determined by the placement of the fabrics. The quilt was finished in the traditional manner.

D

Susan Wilchins
Sunny Side Up

Dyed, screen printed, pieced, appliquéd, stitched; cotton broadcloth, twill; 48 by 48 inches.
Photo: Marc Wilchins

I build my textile pieces through an accumulation of layers on the surface, a type of structure commonly found in the natural world.

I use bright colors and complex textures to re-create the dichotomy I see in nature: compositions which are bold enough to be visible from a distance, but which invite the viewer to come closer and discover an intimate surface alive with texture and visual energy.

C

D

A
Ellen Oppenheimer

Flinderation

Sewn, quilted; commercial
fabrics; 101 by 71 inches.
Photo: Jan Watten

B
Ruth Garrison

Angle of Repose

Painting, piecing, quilting; cotton;
52 by 40 inches.

*Inspired by the southwestern
landscape, this was my first
extensive use of my own painted
fabrics. I enjoy working with the
contrast between the soft color
transitions in paint and the hard
edges of piecing.*

C
Carol Gersen

Rivers in the Sky

Machine piecing, hand quilting;
cotton, Procion dyes; 72 by 72
inches.
Photo: David Caras

D
Jane Reeves

Post Modern XX

Machine piecing, hand quilting;
hand-dyed and commercial
cotton; 64 by 96 inches.

*I am exploring ways to express
illusions of space within a two-
dimensional surface.*

E
Helen Giddens

Mound Man

Machine pieced and quilted;
cotton; 60 by 48 inches.
Photo: Clinton D. Bell

*This piece is about the mound-
builder Indians of the midwest-
ern U.S. I wrote a little of their
history and practices into the
quilt.*

F
Charlotte Yde

*From the Universe of the Snail
- Fossil II*

Machine pieced, hand quilted;
cotton, chintz, silk; 100 by
100 cm.
Photo: Steen Yde

A

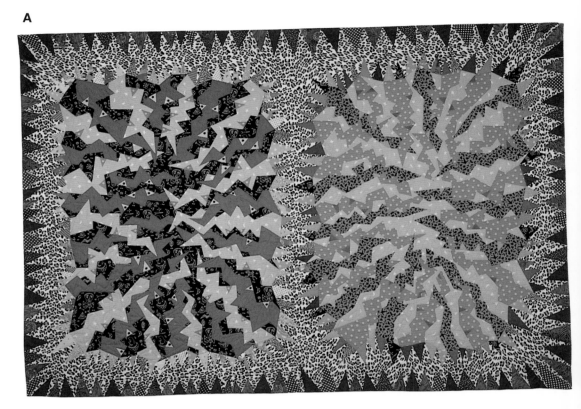

B

C

D

E

F

A

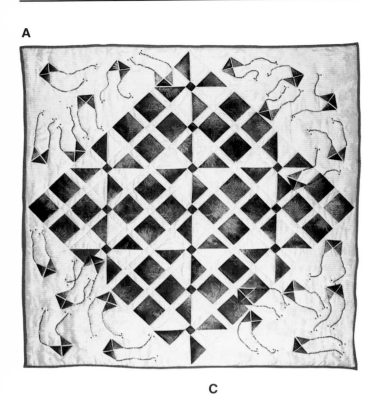

B

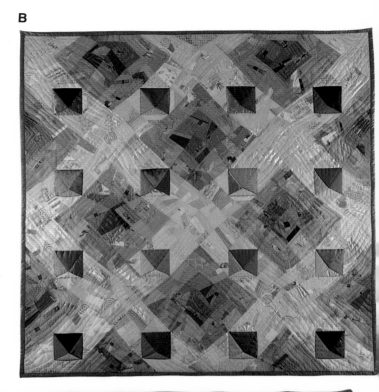

C

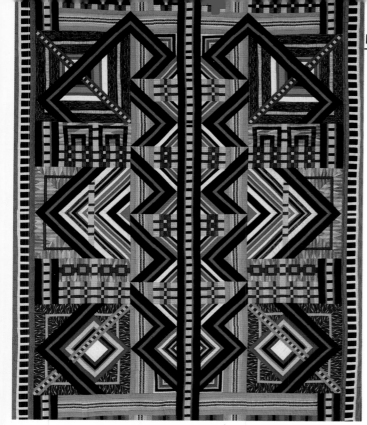

A

H. Jeannette Shanks

Celebration

Machine stitched and quilted; felt, linen, satin, silk; 72 by 74 inches.
Photo: Judith Tinkl

B

Dorle Stern-Straeter

Sandscape

Crazy patchwork, machine piecing, hand quilting; silk, cotton; 1.60 by 1.60 m.
Photo: Patricia Partl

C

Leah Kaspar

Square Study #9

Strip piecing, machine quilting; cotton upholstery and dress fabrics; 108 by 108 inches.
Photo: Walter Plotnick

D

Jenifer Eveleth Fisher

Connections IV - Magic Carpet Ride

Strip and machine piecing, hand quilted; cotton; 58 by 86 inches.
Photo: Greg Plachta Photography

This is a fantasy blanket for touring exotic and mysterious places. It has a soul of its own and is your friend on your travels. Hop on and it gently rises and carries you off for fun and adventure. Come back refreshed, inspired, excited.

E

Paula Nadelstern

Kaleidoscopic III: Stained Glass Anthology

Piecing, quilting; cotton, cotton blends; 72 by 72 inches.
Photo: Bill Aller

The symmetrical repetition of the design, inherent in the kaleidoscope configuration, creates a visual pattern of inferred lines. Some patches connect to their mirror images and act as if reflected so that a plethora of new symmetrical patterns are created…the whole becomes greater than its parts.

Making kaleidoscopes is like making magic with fabric. There is an element of abracadabra as the very last seam is stitched.

E

A

B

C

D

E

F

A

Sally Broadwell

The Fool on the Hill

Piecing, quilting, appliqué, painting; fabric, beads, paint, glitter, found objects; 23 by 19 inches.

B

Clare Murray

Artificial Environment #3

Piecing, appliqué, hand quilting; cotton, cotton blends, hand-dyed fabric; 62 by 68 inches.

C

Miriam Nathan-Roberts

The Museum

Piecing, appliqué, quilting (by Sarah Hershberger); cotton, cotton blends; 58 by 63 inches.

This quilt was a collaboration with my friend Nancy Halpern.

D

Roz Zinns

Cypress St. - Oct. 17

Machine piecing, appliqué and quilting, painting; cotton, nylon, metallics; 58 by 61¼ inches.

The collapse of the Cypress Street superstructure in Oakland, California during the '89 earthquake is visual proof of one's vulnerability to nature's forces.

E

Kathleen Sharp

Vigil

Machine piecing and quilting, hand appliqué; cotton; 50 by 82 inches.
Photo: John Brennan

F

Robin Schwalb

Babel

Silk screen, stencilling, painting, piecing, appliqué, quilting; cotton, paint, beads, thread, batting; 90 by 72 inches.
Photo: Bob Malik Studios

Given my interest in language, the theme of the Tower of Babel is a natural one for me. It also marks a shift away from my earlier, more optimistic work; I question how successfully people can communicate with one another, even when they "speak the same language."

A
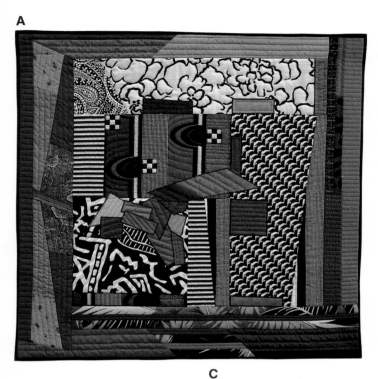

B

C

D

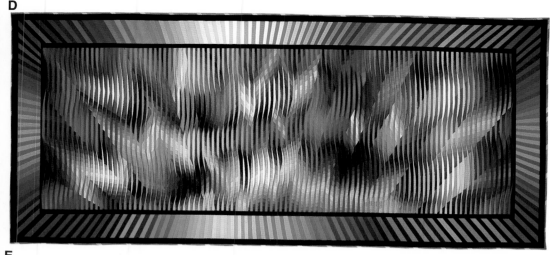

E

A

Esther Parkhurst

Scrap Attack I

Machine piecing and appliqué, hand quilting; cotton; 38 by 38 inches.

I used odd, leftover fabrics from other works and basically let the fabric shapes dictate the structure of the piece.

B

Susan Webb Lee

Screaming Reds

Machine piecing and quilting; cotton; 55½ by 48 inches.
Photo: Steve Budman

C

Ann Brauer

Even in January there is the promise of spring

Piecing, quilting; silk, cotton, muslin; 40 by 55 inches.
Photo: David Caras

A variation on the log cabin pattern.

D

Caryl Bryer Fallert

Aurora II

Dyeing, piecing, pleating, quilting; cotton, wool; 48 by 109 inches.

E

Linda Perry

Soundings

Appliqué, machine piecing, painted, dyed; cotton, silk, metallics; 57 by 70 inches.
Photo: David Caras

My work is influenced by my love of Art Deco and Japanese design.

On occasion I love composing fancy, sitdown dinners with five or six courses and at least two desserts. I cannot abide to follow a recipe. I cook by feel, balancing taste, texture and colors. This is how I quilt.

A

Dottie Moore

Windows

Appliqué, quilting, embroidery; cotton, cotton blends; 70 by 44 inches.
Photo: Image Plus

B

Barbara Lydecker Crane

Sea Change

Piecing, quilting; hand-painted and commercial cotton; 69 by 48 inches.
Photo: David Caras

C

Emily Zopf

Landscape With Houses

Printing, machine piecing and quilting, appliqué; fabric paint, cotton; 63 by 38 inches.

This is a universal landscape. It could be many places in the world and is a reminder of what the people of the world have in common.

D

Carol Anne Grotrian

Pyrotechnics

Shibori, piecing, quilting; hand-dyed and commercial cotton; 59 by 76 inches.
Photo: David Caras

Traditional and non-traditional compass patterns become fireworks over Boston Harbor.

E

Lynn Crook

California Autumn

Machine pieced, hand quilted; cotton; 63 by 63 inches.
Photo: Christopher Crook

I wanted to create a quilt using the colors found around me. The quilting lines carry the theme further by reflecting textures and lines found in nature in the fall leaves and grasses.

A

B

C

D

F

Erika Carter

Timberline

Machine piecing, hand appliqué and quilting; cotton; 49½ by 37 inches.
Photo: Howard Carter

Expressed texturally through color, pattern, piecing and quilting, nature is often the inspiration for my imagery.

E

F

A

Michael James

From the Mountaintop

Machine piecing and quilting;
cotton, silk; 90½ by 68 inches.
Photo: James Beards

*My first quilt that deals with my
response to certain actual
spaces; here, an overlook in the
Swiss Alps. The quality of high
altitude, light, and the particular
way that aspects of the landscape dissolve into haze, giving
a thin, veil-like quality to
otherwise-massive formations,
were considerations in this piece.*

B

Glenne Stoll

Garden Series #2

Strip piecing, channel quilting;
cotton, metallics; 48 by 43
inches.
Photo: Pallas Photo

C

Linda MacDonald

Clear Palisades

Piecing, dyeing, hand quilting;
cotton, Procion dye; 92 by 92
inches.
Photo: Sharon Risedorph.

*The challenge is to create the
illusion of three-dimensional
landscapes that transcend the
expected and foray into new
experiences.*

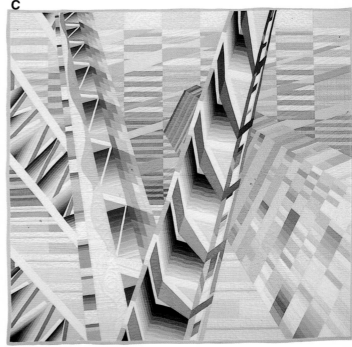

D

D

Wendy Lewington Coulter

Teacup Aunties

Machine piecing, appliqué, hand quilting, embroidery, painting, dyeing; hand-dyed and commercial fabric, beads, buttons, metallics; 120 by 154 cm. Photo: White Museum of the Canadian Rockie

This quilt is a portrait of my great aunts Rosa Atkins and Elsie Bell who gave generously from their china teacup collections every birthday and Christmas from when I was 13 till 21.

E

Sally Broadwell

Tiger, Tiger Burning Bright

Piecing, quilting, appliqué, painting; fabric, beads, paint, glitter, found objects; 23 by 19 inches.

E

A

Ursula Gerber-Senger

Polarity

Hand pieced and quilted; kork-skin, hand spun and woven silk; 72 by 57 inches.
Photo: Thomas Cugini

B

Roxana Bartlett

And Shadows Hold Their Breath

Dyeing, piecing, painting, appliqué, hand quilting; cotton, acetate satin, Procion dye, ink; 59 by 59 inches.
Photo: Ken Sanville

This image is like those feelings which enter through the senses; they move through our hearts and minds as dreams. The tides of the seasons and the rhythms of the hours are important in my work, seemingly inevitable to symbolize the passage of time and lives.

B

A

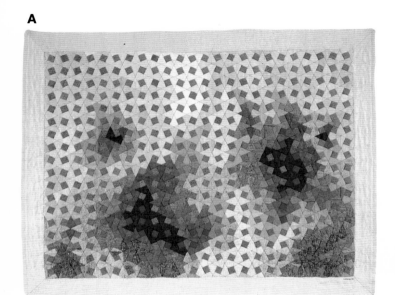

C

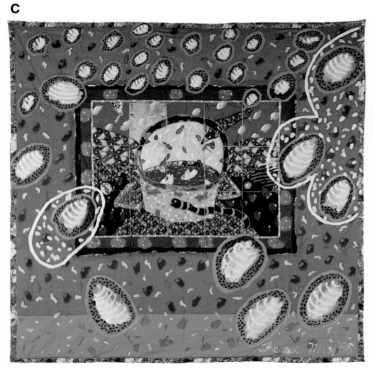

D

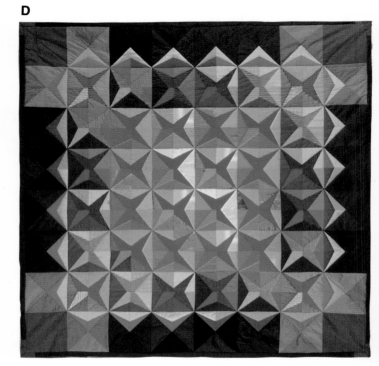

C
Therese May
Basket

Machine appliqué; various
fabrics, acrylic paint; 84 by
84 inches.
Photo: Curtis Fukuda

*I start out with a drawing as
a pattern to cut the fabric. The
pieces are pinned to a muslin
backing and then machine appliquéd. I do not cut my threads;
instead I let them form a net-
work-like texture over the surface of the quilt.*

D
Schnuppe von Gwinner
Apple of Paradise

Patchwork, hand quilted; cotton,
silk; 200 by 220 cm.
Photo: Karsten Mueller

*The name for this quilt was
coined by my father.*

E
Julie von der Ropp
Heraldic With A Green Kick

Hand pieced; cotton, acetate
blends; 37 by 37 inches.
Photo: Ingo Serej Kischnik

E

A

Erika Odemer

Color Eruption

Hand quilted; cotton, silk, dyed;
78½ by 78½ inches.
Photo: Patricia Partl

*This is my rather complicated
way of working with the Log
Cabin technique.*

B

Carol Westfall

Crazy Quilt II

Stitchery, collage, computer-
generated design; silk, paper,
paint, fiber glass; 42 by 60
inches.
Photo: Will Brown

*This "quilt" will never keep any-
one warm, but it is great fun to
see, touch and think about.*

C

Cherry Partee

Coverlet

Quilted, painted; pigment on silk;
43 by 64 inches.
Photo: Ken Wagner

*I have been thinking about the
quilt as metaphor for women's
lives, of how it can reveal and
conceal, comfort or suffocate.
A picture of a thing in our culture
is often more valuable than the
thing portrayed. The image of
women as shown in the media,
in romantic novels, in advertising
seems to be more real and valuable than the person herself.
This piece is about self identity.*

A

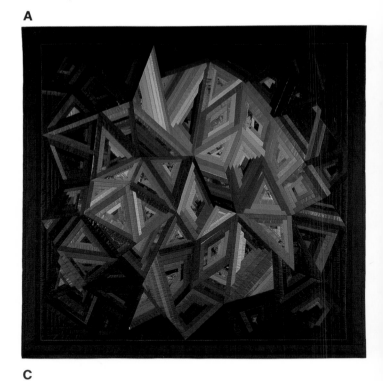

C

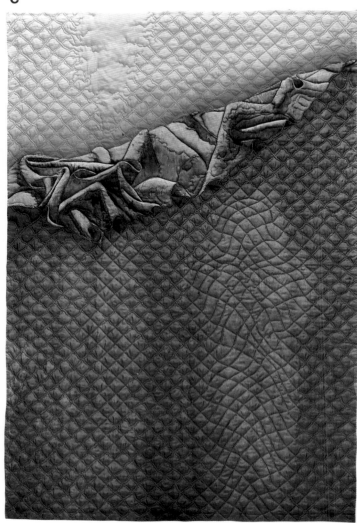

B

102

Maribeth Baloga
Ebikhil

Embroidery; cotton, muslin, colored pencils; 6¼ by 6¼ inches.
Photo: Taunton Press

A

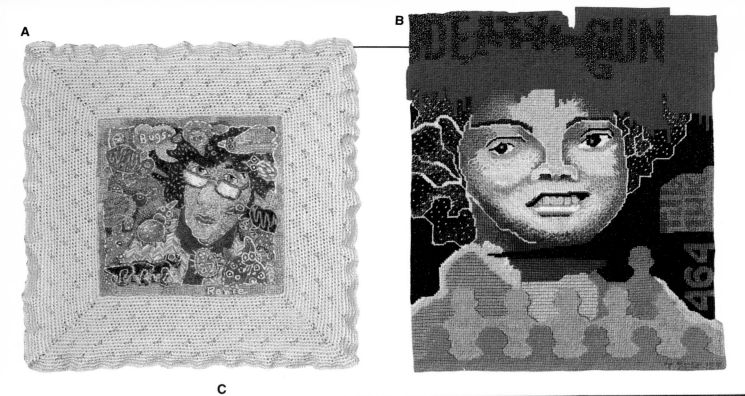

B

C

D

E

A

Renie Breskin Adams

Bugs

Embroidery, crochet; cotton; 6½ by 6½ inches.

B

Theodora Zehner

Death Gun

Petit point, 576 stitches per square inch; cotton, metallics; 9¼ by 9 inches.
Photo: James Lentini

Using a computer, I scanned and manipulated a TIME magazine cover. A computer printout was made, followed by several hand drawings to help establish the basic composition. The color application is instinctive and the glow-in-the-dark yarn afterimage, a touch of irony.

C

Jonni Turner

Th'bee is a SPIRIT

Petit point, appliqué, needleweaving, crochet; cotton, silk; 8 by 6⅞ inches.
Photo: Lee Atkinson

This is a work based on the poems of Canadian Joe Rosenblatt. The bee is a spirit of nature enticing the jaded lovers back to the garden.

D

Mary Bero

Graffiti Still Life

Embroidery, knitting, appliqué; cotton, rayon; 10 by 8 inches.
Photo: Jim Wildeman

E

Theodora Elston

Japan

Embroidery, painting; silk, cotton, acrylic paint; 15 by 17 inches.

This is part of a series in the spirit of "having fun, wish you were here!" travel postcards.

A

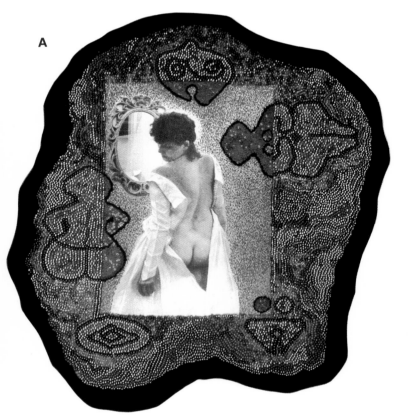

B

C

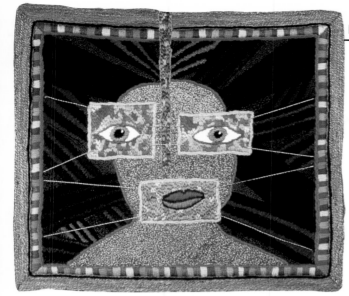

D

A

Mary Ann Hickey

Return To The Goddess

Embroidery, beading, appliqué, heat transfer; beads, heat-transferred image, ultrasuede; 11¾ by 11 by 1¼ inches.
Photo: Joe Hirsch

Trying on my wedding gown (more than 30 years and 30 pounds later) provided the experience for this piece.

Early Christianity's devotion to the virgin was derived from patri-archal appropriation of goddess imagery. Combining my personal history with goddess imagery is my way of reclaiming this source of power for women.

B

Sandra Nickeson

Taking It On the Chin: A 1990 Sampler

Stitching; silk, rayon and metallic threads; antique photograph, linen; 13¼ by 15¾ inches.
Photo: Red Elf, Inc.

My work is about rhythm, relationships, continuity with the past…the stuff beneath the skin of life. I follow the dictum of Anais Nin: "create against destruction."

C

Caroline Dahl

Rome Under Water

Embroidery; cotton; 26 by 20 inches.
Photo: Faulkner Color Lab

D

Julianna Mahley

It Isn't Mary

Embroidery; cotton and metallic thread; 7½ by 6½ inches.

I am fascinated with the various masks, facades and ambiguities inherent in our lives.

E

Mary Bero

Jungle Fusion

Embroidery, knotting, appliqué; cotton, lace, rayon; 4¾ by 8⅜ inches.
Photo: Jim Wildeman

E

A

B

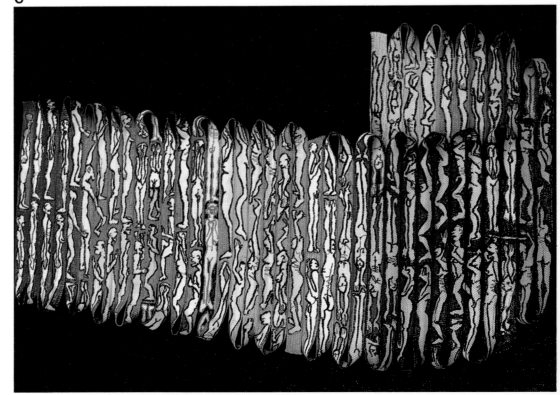

C

A
Tilleke Schwarz

In Memoriam

Embroidery; cotton, silk, linen; 73 by 63 cm.

I learned to embroider from my mother, but when I went to art academies, I discovered there was no interest in this elaborate and feminine technique. Nevertheless, I kept making embroideries as I felt that everyone has a right to some aberration.

B
Anna Torma

The Field

Embroidery; cotton, linen, silk; 78 by 75 cm.

C
Susanne Klinke

Cut

Machine embroidery; webbing, cotton floss; 82 by 52 cm.

D
Elly Smith

Embroidery As the Leisure Art

Counted thread cross stitch and back stitch; even-weave linen, cotton and metallic thread; 27 by 57 inches.
Photo: Steve Meltzer

The format is like contemporary sampler—many motifs scattered everywhere; some mystery, some lettering, historical references, etc.

The realization of the woman stitching her sampler is about time. The hand above her head indicates my desire to incorporate the past (through old needlework motifs) with the present. This design resulted from having read Rozsika Parker's book, The Subservice Stitch.

D

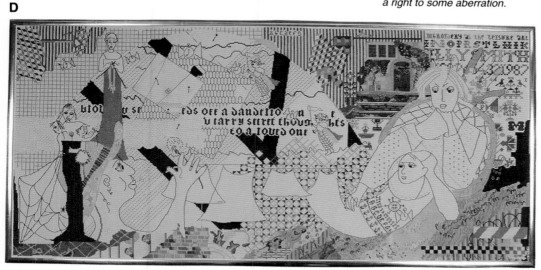

E
Erma Martin Yost

Spirit Pass

Assemblage, machine piecing, quilting and embroidering; canvas, cyanotype; 38 by 32 inches.
Photo: Courtesy Noho Gallery, NYC

I hand paint or hand print the fabrics, then cut them up and machine embroider them before assembly.

The imagery refers to the American Southwest where I spent considerable time seeking ancient rock paintings left by the Indians. A strong sense of place exists at these sites. They are places of ritual and ceremony, the essence of which I tried to capture in this piece.

E

A

Dianne Dennis

Lovers' Knots

Needlepoint; cotton; 9¼ by 9¼ inches.

My love of quilts and color, and my background in weaving all come together in this piece.

B

Barbara Lee Smith

Light/Storm

Machine embroidery; cotton, silk, rayon; 32 by 23 inches.
Photo: Mark A. Smith

C

Paulette Peroni

Pisces

Embroidery; wool; 1 by 1½ m.
Photo: Paladino.

This stitch (imitating weaving but needle-embroidered) captures light well and is easier and quicker than classical petit point or cross stitch.

D

Julia A. Walsh

Communion of Love

Drawn thread work, knotting; French tapestry fabric, cotton floss; 47 by 40 inches.
Photo: Karl VanBurkleo

E

Tilleke Schwarz

Where is the cat?

Embroidery; cotton, silk, linen; 76 by 68 cm.

A

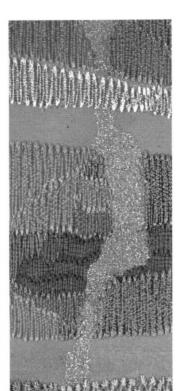

B

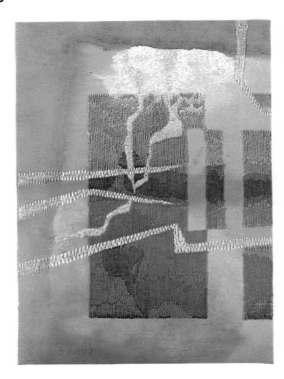

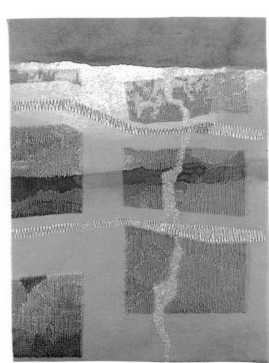

C

D

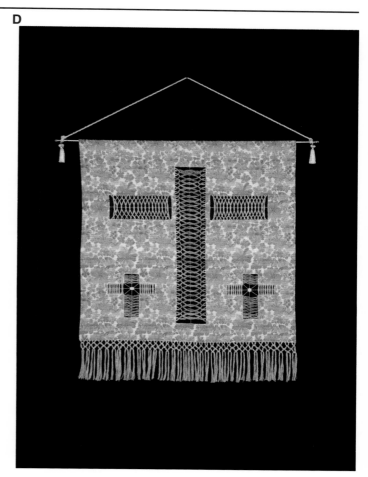

E

A
Beth Nobles
Dairy Queen

Embroidery; cotton; 3 by
6 inches.
Photo: Jon Van Allen

*I grew up on old Route 66 in
Illinois. We were close enough
to the highway that we could
look past the cornfield near our
house and see the cars passing.
My seat at the dining room table
gave me a clear view of the road.
I figure I ate 8,000 meals looking
at that stretch of highway.
Bob Johnson's restaurant had
an enormous plastic chicken on
its roof; westbound drivers could
see the feature as they passed.
Not too far off the highway was
the Dairy Queen, the Steak and
Shake, and the Dog 'n' Suds,
where you could still get curb-
side service and baby mugs of
root beer.*

   *We are slowly letting our old
roadside culture get bulldozed.
I did this piece because I want
people to appreciate the one
building from this dying culture
that is still left. Our Dairy Queen
has the most gorgeous neon
lights that turn every trip there
into a theatrical experience. It is
just not the same as going to the
mall for a Baskin-Robbins. I'm
grateful we still have the choice.*

B
Nancy Martineau
Loveseat

Traditional rug hooking; wool,
wool blends; 48 by 36 inches.
Photo: Jed Eli

*This is a lighthearted look at a
most misunderstood animal.
I like to think that something
I have created might add a bit
of whimsy to an otherwise
dreary day.*

C
Patricia Weller
Planarian Birthday Book

Punch needle embroidery;
cotton, acrylic, wool, linen;
16 by 16 by 2 inches.

*Many of my construction tech-
niques are derived from a fly
fishing tying class which I took
specifically to learn skills and
find materials I could apply to
my artwork.*

   *My images are visual abstrac-
tions of events or issues in my
life. Sometimes painful, I nevertheless deal with them in a
humorous way.*

D

Tom Lundberg

Planting

Embroidery; cotton, silk,
metallics on wool canvas;
3½ inches diam.
Photo: Colorado State University
Photographic Services

E

Janet Leszczynski

Threshold: Passing Through

Embroidery; cotton; 3¼ by 2⅞
inches.
Photo: Steve Grubman

*I work to create worlds where
my dreams and whimsy may be
played out.*

C

D

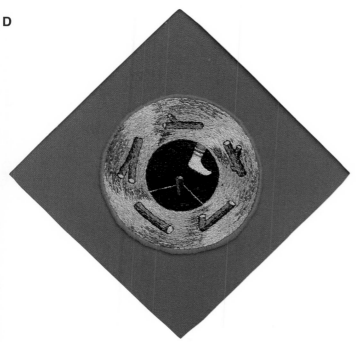

E

A

B

C

D

E

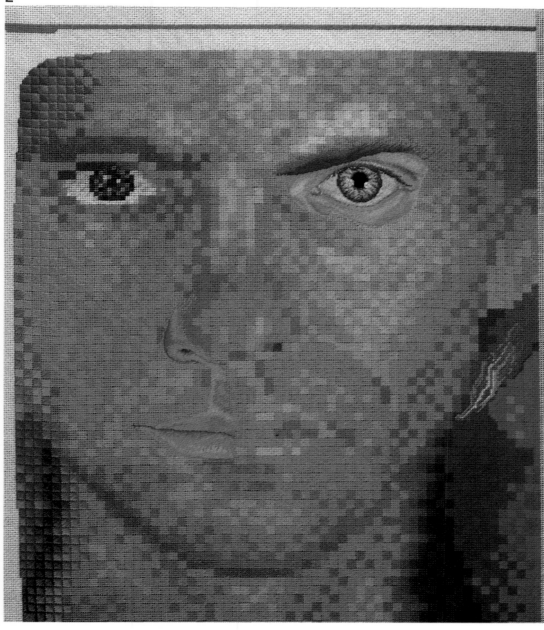

A

Belinda Raab

Cornhead the Barbarian

Needlepoint, tent stitch; silk, cotton; 8 by 10¼ inches. Photo: Wayne Raab

B

Helene Volfikova

Prague Motif

Bobbin lace; flax; 54½ by 41⅕ cm.

C

Natacha Wolters

Mosaiques

Bead embroidery, petit point, bargello, painting; glass and metal beads, silk and wool threads, cotton; 64 by 55 cm.

D

Emily Marks

Royal Teapot

Crochet, sewing, glueing; yarn, imitation pearls; 10 by 10 by 6 inches.

E

Jonni Turner

Dreams of the Computer: Realization

Petit point, appliqué, stitching; cotton, silk; 13½ by 11¼ inches. Photo: Lee Atkinson

"Realization" is part of a series based on human nightmares about computers from the computer's point of view. It makes a statement not only about depersonalization, but about the potential for using computers for intellectual growth.

A

Madeleine Colaco

Palmeiras Do Para

Needlework, Brazilian stitch;
wool, silk, cotton; 130 by 188 cm.
Photo: Jorge Colaco

B

Eleanor Parise

Argentine Birds

Crewel, surface stitchery; cotton,
wool, dyed fibers; 35 by 24
inches.
Photo: Rudolf Parise

*The three human races are
represented, united before a
common divinity, in this case
The Sun Temple.*

*The piece was created using
a series of photographs taken
in the forests of northeastern
Argentina, near Eldorado.*

A

B

Two Dimensions

Morgan Clifford
Bites
Weft brocade; linen, silk; 20 by
20 inches.
Photo: Peter Lee

*My work was once described as
a cross between early American
samplers, Aboriginal cave paintings and high tech. I like that.*

A

Margaret Cusack

SSMC Products on Clouds

Collage, dyeing; satin, cotton;
19 by 15 inches.

B

Roslyn Logsdon

Italian Conversation

Rug hooking; wool; 39 by 30
inches.
Photo: Linda Zandler

C

Deidre Scherer

Time Span

Piecing, layering, machine stitching; cotton; 7½ by 7 inches.

*Up to a certain point, I am in
control, then I follow a "sense
of being."*

A

B

C

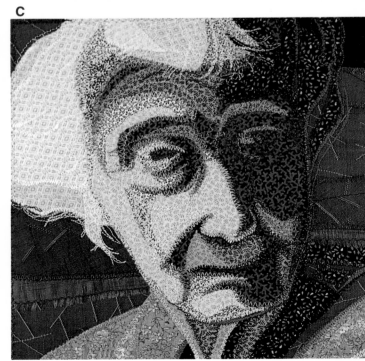

D

Katarina Zavarska

Brothers

Weaving, sewing; wool, photo transfer, hemp; 110 by 110 cm.

Something positive and lasting comes from fine-woven, selected details. The relationship between subjective and objective reality creates a complete unity.

E

Susan Sternlieb

After School

Weft faced rag tapestry; cotton, cotton blends; 34 by 30 inches. Photo: CSU Photo Services

F

James Gilbert

Japan

Woven, silkscreen, painted; cotton, rayon, lurex, ink; 44 by 52 inches.

The red circle is Japan's flag insignia and symbolizes Japan internationally. It also represents a warm, glowing sun that has radiated over Japan for many centuries.

The two body images symbolize the large islands of Japan, floating in a gigantic sea. The maiden's shape is symbolic of the swooping arc of the largest Japanese island.

E

F

A

Karen Chapnick

Close Proximity

Interlocking braiding; painted
fabric; 84 by 52 inches.
Photo: Barbara Cohen

B

John Skau

Ripple Effect

Tufting, lamination, painting,
embroidery; wool, liquid plastic,
rug canvas; 69 by 41 inches.

*Shrinking carpet? Effects from
that bottle of Ripple? Nope...it's
a trompe l'oeil!*

C

Fran Cutrell Rutkovsky

Occupant

Weaving, collage; junk mail,
brochures, photocopies, cotton;
22 by 16⅛ inches.
Photo: Richard Brunck

*"Occupant" refers to the deluge
of promotional materials, usually
unwanted, that are designed to
attract consumers.*

D

Lynne Sward

Hide and Seek

Machine and hand sewn; cotton,
cotton blends, metallic fabrics;
27 by 9 inches.

A

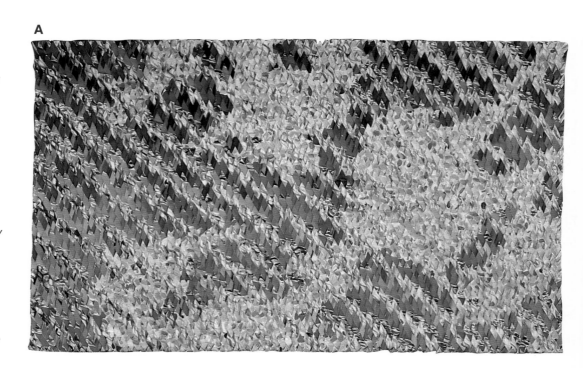

B

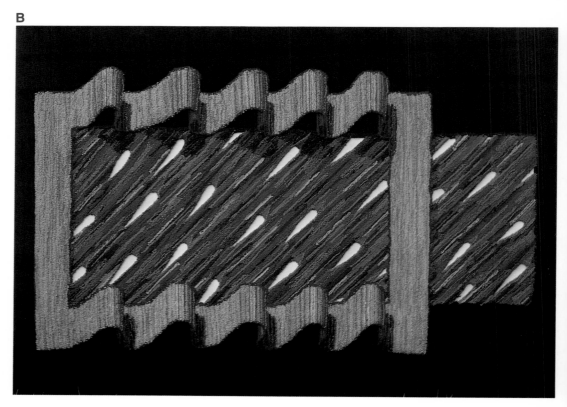

C

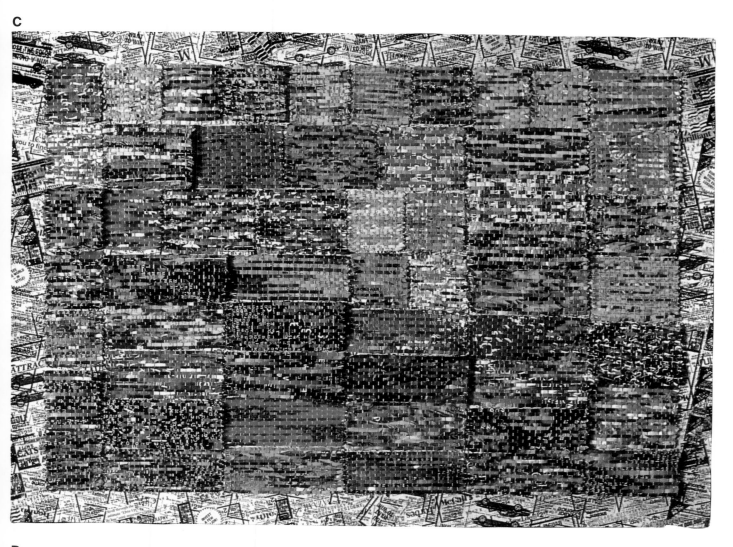

D

A

Joyce Marquess Carey

Dragon Robes

Appliqué, reverse appliqué, embroidery; satin, jacquard-woven portraits, found objects; 57 by 36 inches.

Chairman Mao is dressed as he might appear in different periods of history. First, he wears a Mandarin "dragon" robe, then an "alligator" bathrobe. Last, Mao the tourist wears a dinosaur-print sportshirt.

B

Jacqueline Treloar

The Angel with the Superscription

Painting, heat transfer, stitching; nylon, silk organza, canvas, acrylic and textile paints, ribbons, beads; 108 by 88 inches.

Photo: Allison Oulette

The central angel in the piece is one of 10 on the Ponte Sant'Angelo in Rome. It is of painted canvas backed with mylar. The back layer of the hanging, which is nylon, is finished with an open web effect in silver and gold paint. The two larger angels are appliquéd onto the front of this layer.

C

Jeannie Kamins

Portrait of George Szanto

Machine appliqué, painting; mixed fabric, oil paint; 39 by 51 inches.
Photo: Henri Robideau

Szanto is a writer who lives in Mexico. Both he and I have been significantly influenced by Mexican muralist Orozco.

D

Katherine Knauer

Flying Cadet, 1943

Crazy quilt, embroidery, stencilling, appliqué, piecing, punchneedle, painting; luxury fabrics, canvas, found objects; 67 by 67 inches.
Photo: Gamma One

This piece attempts to blur the distinction between painting and quiltmaking. The only section that is actually quilted is the painted portion.

C

D

A

Susanne Klinke

Forever

Assemblage, embroidery; paper, pigments, cotton and silk threads; 23 by 16 cm.

B

Rosita Johanson

Hungarian Revolution

Machine appliqué, machine and hand embroidery; cotton, metallic thread, wrist watch parts; 5⅜ by 5½ inches.
Photo: Lenscape Inc.

C

Linda Laino

Gates of Faith

Tapestry, embroidery, painting; wool, linen, felt, cotton, paint; 40 by 48 inches.

D

Elaine Polvinen

Spirituality; Woman Inside, Her Soul, Fig. 1

Weaving, airbrush; silk tussah, dye; 43 by 60 inches.

E

Laura Brody

Maelstrom

Warp painted linen, inlay; linen, cotton, pigment; 60 by 40 inches.

A

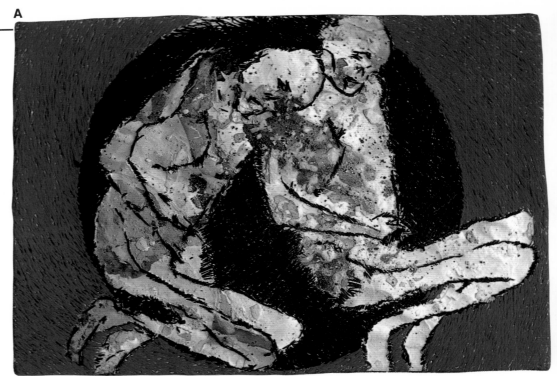

B

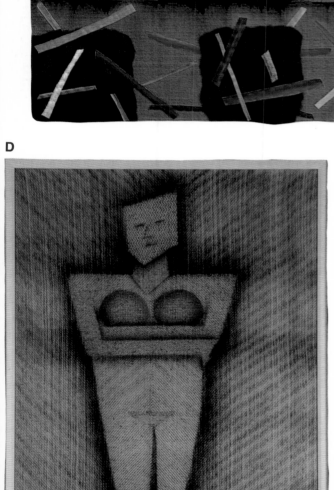

D

E

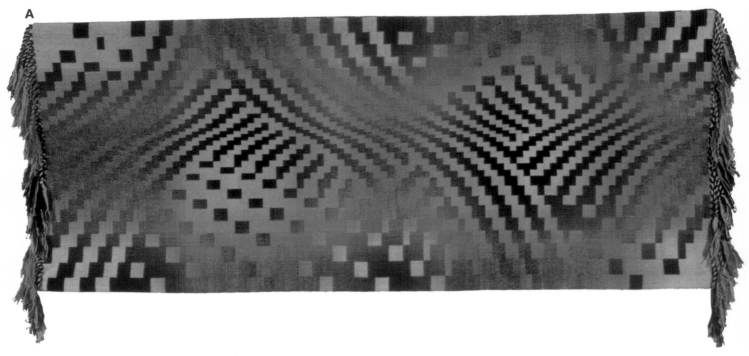

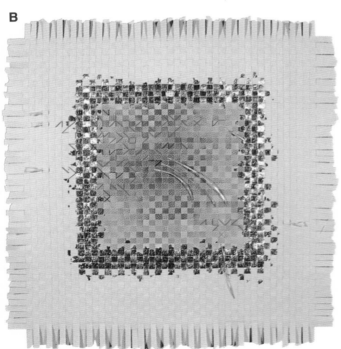

D

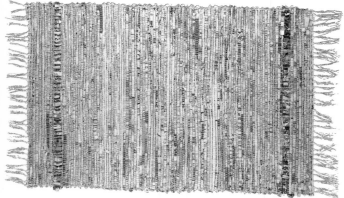

A

Jean Davies Nordlund

Lightworks II

Double-weave; wool; 120 by 48 inches.
Photo: TAI

B

Alice Van Leunen

The Invention of Poetry

Airbrush, stitchery, weaving; paper, foil, watercolor, cotton; 37 by 36 inches.

The work I specialize in is almost invariably tedious, painstaking and time-consuming, probably the result of bad karma…

C

Martin Baker

Spring Thaw

Tapestry (woven by Fausto Contreras); wool, acrylic, dye; 52 by 74 inches.

D

Joan Rothenmeyer Hutten

Rag Run-Sunday, October 22

Woven; cotton, newspaper; 34 by 20½ inches.
Photo: Joel Becker

The piece is part of my "Cash for Trash" series. The title refers to the technique as well as the slang, rag, for a newspaper.

E

Elizabeth Fiset

Diamonds on the Souls

Flat weave; wool, linen; 36 by 60 inches.

F

Olga Rothschild

Straight Furrow

Hand hooking, dyeing; linen, wool; 42 by 54 inches.
Photo: Pictures of Record, Inc.

E

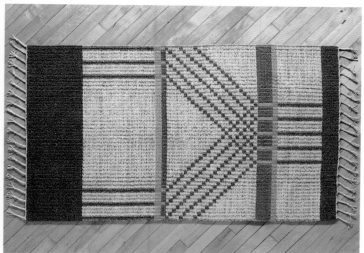

F

A

B

C

D

A

Maria Skochova

Darkness Full of Lights

Art-protis tapestry; wool, tulle;
130 by 180 cm.

B

Lucy Jahns

Inspiration

Machine embroidery, appliqué,
dyeing; cotton, sailcloth, dye;
71 by 41 inches.

C

Dominie Nash

Sky Song

Appliqué, overlays, machine
quilting, silkscreen, dyeing; cotton, silk, dyes, textile pigments,
fleece; 70 by 43 inches.

*I'm interested in the depth and
color changes which are created
by layering transparent over
opaque fabric.*

D

Gayle Anderson

Pele's Watching

Inking, assemblage; handmade
paper, acrylic paint, found metal;
24 by 29 inches.
Photo: Malama Arts, Inc.

*This is a comment on the pollu-
tion (rusted metal) on the island
of Kailua-Kona. The goddess
Pele looks on.*

A

Patricia Malarcher

Border Incident

Machine stitching, painting, sewing; canvas, mylar, linen; 72 by 60 inches.
Photo: D. James Dee

B

Dora Hsiung

Dawn to Dusk

Wrapping, layering; rug wool; 96 by 60 inches.

C

Joyce Crain

Manhattan Amnesia

Interlacing, collage; film, metallic braids, acetate gels, plastic netting; 36 by 48 by 3 inches.
Photo: Becket Logan

D

Nancy Herman

4 Part Harmony

Weaving, piecing; mixed fibers; 72 by 60 inches.
Photo: Ken Kauffman

I want to release light through sequences of color, pattern, and texture interacting. I am interested in "playing" these different "instruments" together to increase the musicality of the piece.

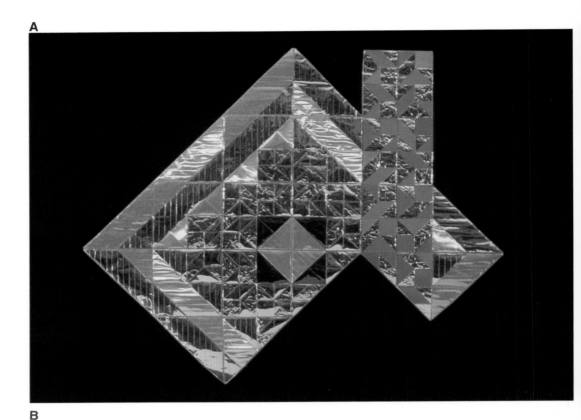

C

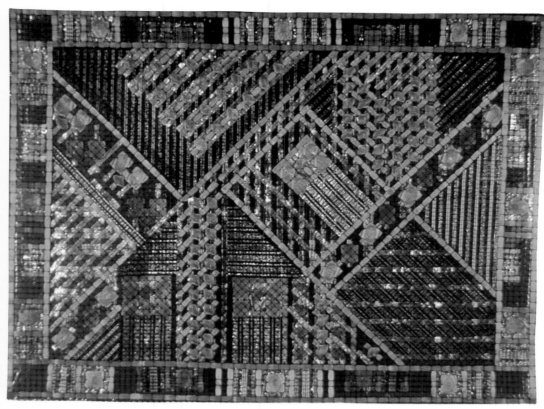

D

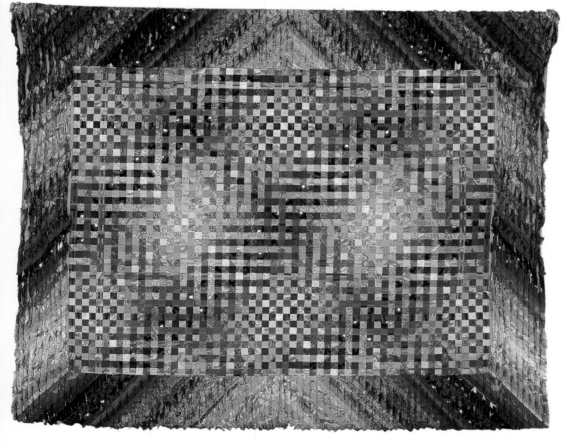

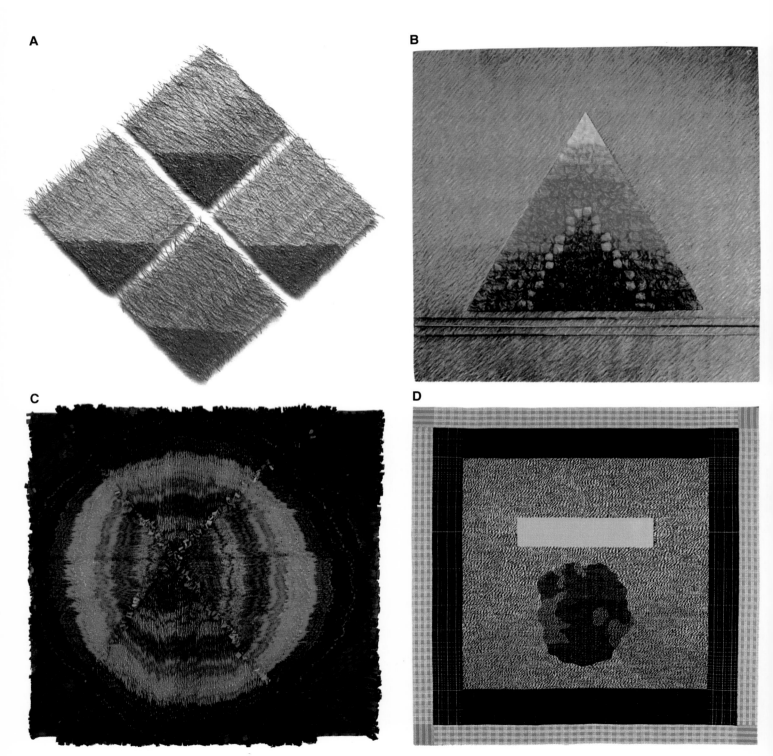

A
Lis Gram

Pompidou

Stripping, sewing; plastic bags, Plexiglas; 100 by 100 cm.

B
Louisa Simons

In the Beginning was Color

Painting, shirring; silk, fiber reactive dye; 1100 by 1100 mm.

C
Judith Larzelere

Cross Section

Machine piecing, stitching; cotton; 77 by 76 inches.
Photo: Bindas Studio, Boston

I search for images of great simplicity that can elicit a variety of responses from viewers.

D
Claire Campbell Park

Koi II

Woven; linen, cotton, metallic thread; 61 by 61 inches.
Photo: Robin Stancliff.

I think of the area of solid color as a window to another reality, and the area of fractured color as energy and light.

E
Ann Sinclair

Morning Has Broken II

Shadow weave, inlay; cotton, wool, rayon; 24 by 26½ inches.

F
Merrill Mason

Tornado I

Machine piecing and embroidery, stamping, sewing; cotton, polyester, Xerox transfer, textile pigments, buttons, beads; 49 by 48½ inches.
Photo: Eric Landsberg

I like to make quilts using unlikely subject matter. Hopefully, the quilt format draws people in with expectations of beauty, comfort and domesticity. The format makes them less resistant to ideas they might otherwise shun.

E

F

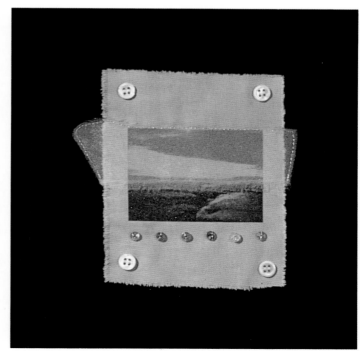

A

A

Emily DuBois

Approach

Computer-aided weaving, ikat dyeing; cotton; 130 by 54 inches.

I use dyeing and weaving to suggest natural forces, like the rippling waves in water or patterns in shells.

B

Joan Hausrath

Dawn

Dipped, dyed, warp faced; wool; 72 by 40 inches.

B

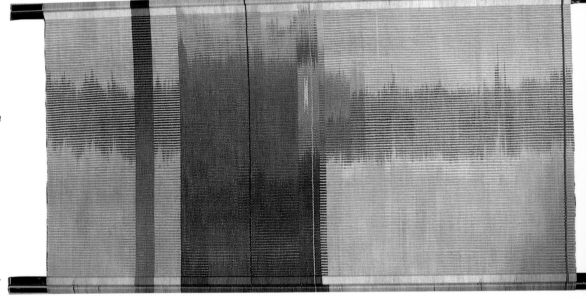

C

Ann Epstein

Fun-Loving But Not Anti-Intellectual

Ikat-dyed and woven; cotton; 69 by 45 inches.
Photo: Larime Photographic

My work generally deals abstractly with universal human emotional states—expressed via color and texture—as I am also a psychologist.

D

Kay Cheever

Magic Mountain Blues

Weaving, dyeing; Georgia rug wool, dyes; 29 by 29 inches.

I am an amateur horticulturist and enjoy using natural dyes. I do not strive for evenness of color, preferring the kinetic, light-flickering quality and subtle differences of dye not perfectly applied.

C

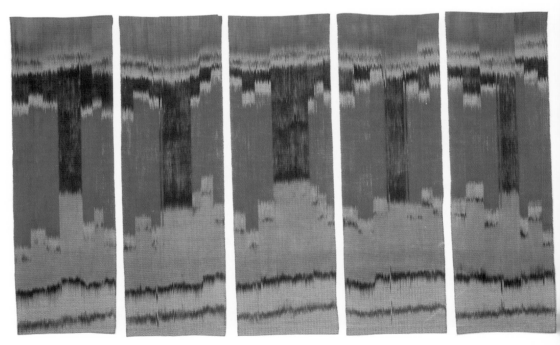

E

Cameron Taylor-Brown

Triplication/Splashdown
[one of three pieces]

Supplemental warp brocade, wrapped on painted wooden frames; linen, cotton, rayon, metallics, nylon netting; 64 by 184 inches total, each unit 50 by 54 inches.
Photo: Clique Studios

F

Mary Tyler

China Gate

Warp woven, space dyed; silk; 68 by 71 inches.

G

Louise Lemieux Berube

Light & Shadow #156

Shadow weave; CAD-aided; rayon, metallics; 40 by 40 inches.

D

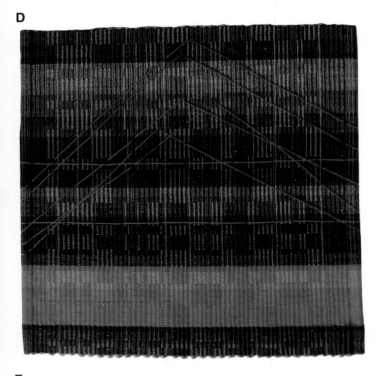

E

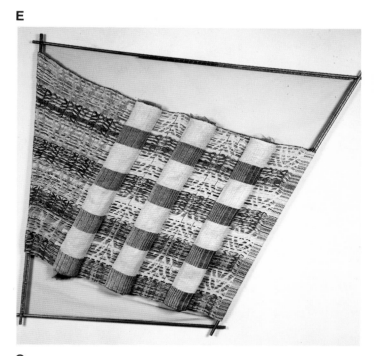

F

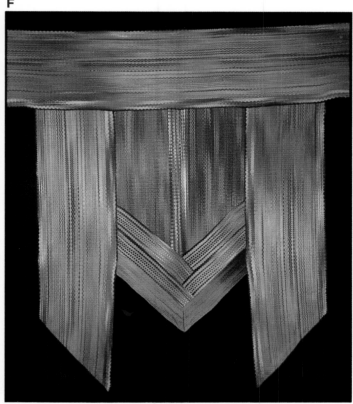

G

A

Jeff Glenn

All Summer Swim

Painted, woven double warp;
cotton, rayon, canvas, felt, dye;
52 by 57 inches.
Photo: Gary Sinick

B

Jeff Glenn

Twists and Turns

Painted, woven triple warp;
cotton, linen, rayon, felt,
canvas, dye.
Photo: Jay Graham

C

Janet Ecklebarger

Untitled

Double weave pick up; hand-
dyed silk, cotton; 28½ by 36
inches.

*I am fascinated with the role
textiles play in tribal cultures.*

D

Rena Thompson

Lilah's Light

Double weave pickup; wool;
85 by 51 inches.

E

Jennifer Moore

Storm Warning

Double weave pickup; cotton;
37½ by 30 inches.
Photo: Bill Dewey

A

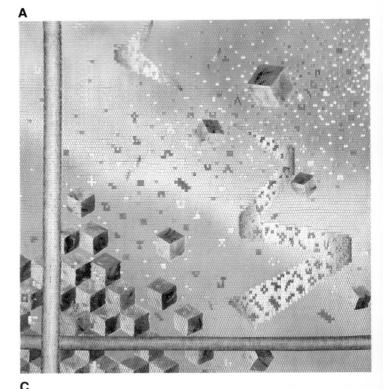

C

B

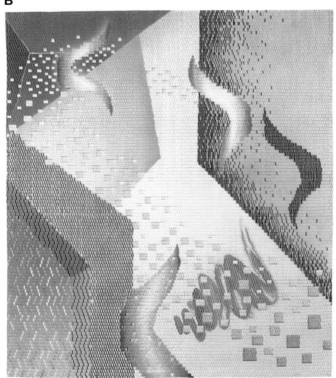

D

E

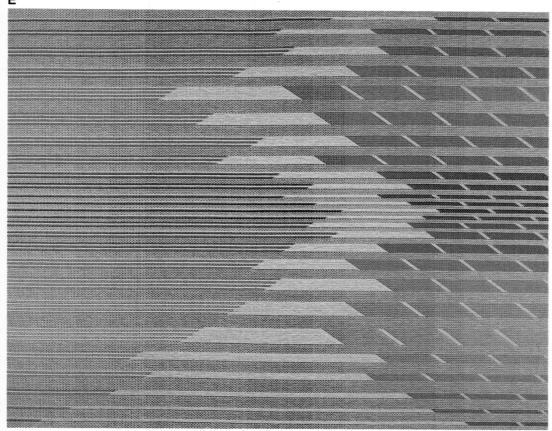

A

Annemarie Buchmann-Gerber

Fish Queue

Painted tapestry, appliqué, collage, stitchery; rayon, acrylic paint, cotton; 146 by 122 cm. Photo: Louise Barak

B

Rosa Vercaemst

On the Contrary

Bobbin lace; cotton; 80 by 80 cm.

In my textile compositions, I concentrate on showing the very soul of lace—its transparency. I want to keep far away from technical acrobacy and sophistication.

C

Anita Berman

Driftnet 1990

Tapestry, wrapping, watercolor; rayon, metallic yarn, dye; 15 by 15 cm.

This work reflects my concern about the threat to many fish species because of the driftnet fishing in the Pacific.

D

Robin Schwalb

Introductory Japanese

Machine piecing, hand appliqué and quilting, stencilling; cotton, embroidery thread; 45 by 45 inches.

Anticipating the calligraphic beauty of the signs in Tokyo, I was shocked to see the large amount of English used everywhere. However, I quickly discovered how fractured English a la Japanese is.

A

B

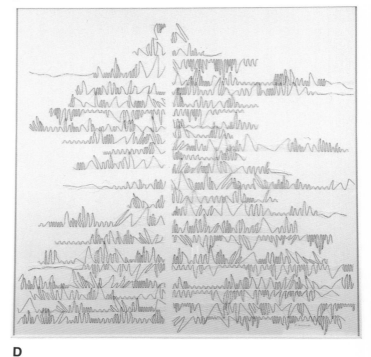

C

D

E

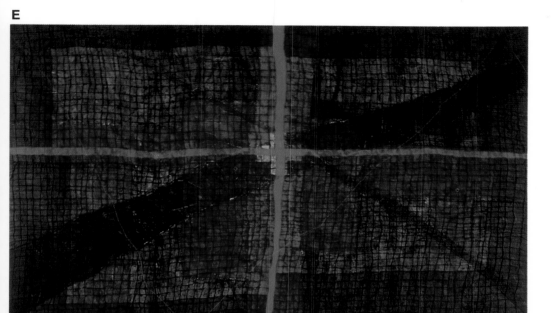

Erica Licea-Kane

Crossroads

Layering, painting; fabric, dental floss, acrylics, net; 48 by 84 inches.
Photo: Gordon Bernstein

F

Barbara Oliver Hartman

Sounds: A Hot Summer Night

Appliqué, embroidery; cotton; 57 by 76 inches.

This is a free form composition designed in a spontaneous manner. Shapes represent sound and colors represent heat.

G

Valerie Hearder

African Skirt Series V: Tropic of Capricorn

Hand appliqué, piecing; cotton, taffeta, sequins; 28 by 36 inches.

By making reference to the traditional shapes of the Ndebele skirts, I felt I was tapping into an ancient cultural awareness. Here was the format I've been seeking to express my political thoughts and spirituality.

G

F

A

Donna Durbin

The Messengers

Double weave pick up; cotton, linen; 32 by 31 inches.

This is my attempt to create an energized astral space in which the future is sending warnings to the present about the preservation of our planet.

B

Fuyuko Matsubara

The Crystal in the Air I

Painted warp and weft, inlay, double weave; linen, cotton, ramie, silk, rayon; 88 by 58 inches.

A crystal is growing in the air of the inner world where everything is made of light. The light reflects and forms images. One of them is the metamorphosis of oneself. There is a spiral line that separates the inner world and this world. Close to the line is where words exist. There is an area where natural objects are transforming. This symbolizes our immediate environment and appears focused to us.

C

Randal Crawford

Time Map

Double weave pickup, painting, dyeing; cotton, rayon; 48 by 75 inches.
Photo: David Dreher

The concept of journey is the basis of my investigation. Weaving is my means of recording information and of drawing the path with threads. I am plotting shapes within the given space and finding new relationships as I continue. The cloth holds the memory of the experience.

D

Mi-Young Moon

A Salute to Fall

Weaving; cotton; 41½ by 74 inches.
Photo: Lee Man-Hong

The imagery involves ideas as personal metaphors. The warp threads are ikated and then woven in a supplementary warp pick up technique. Each thread is individually brought to the surface as I select it rather than programmed into the loom in a pattern weave.

A

B

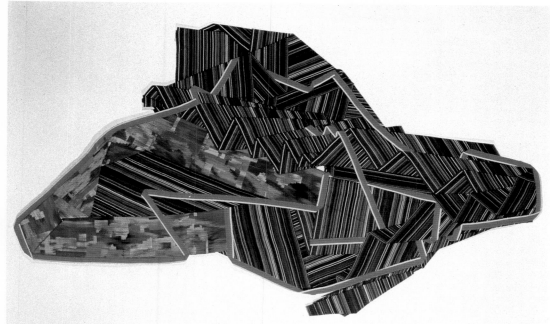

E

Barbara Schulman
Twist of Gait
Woven; pulled warp; cotton,
linen; 32 by 22½ inches.
Photo: Doug Van de Zande

D

E

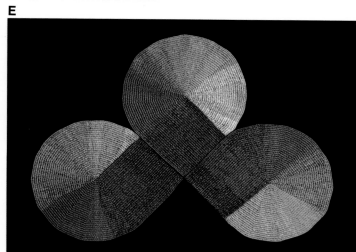

A

W. Logan Fry

Ancient Maze

Merino wool; Finnweave; 10 by
12 inches.
Photo: Jean Schnell

*The piece is nearly architec-
tural—like the foundations of an
ancient city or the plan for a
maze in a formal English garden.*

B

Gail Skudera

Satin Five Patch

Painted canvas, weaving; cotton,
acrylic paint; 144 by 48 inches.

*A restaurant lounge with a
famous view of Chicago commissioned the piece. It was an excit-
ing challenge to work within the
dictates of architectural design
and colors.*

C

Carol Jessen

Autumn Flight

Appliqué, xerography, tulle over-
lay; fabric, paper; 33 by 23
inches.

*I have always thought that birds
in flight are truly poetic in motion.
Stroboscopic photography was
used to capture the image and
repetition of it creates an imag-
ined flock.*

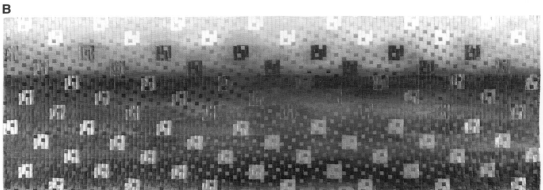

D

D

Patricia Malarcher

Untitled Hanging for St. Cecilia's Church

Machine stitching, sewing; mylar, fabric, linen; 84 by 120 inches. Photo: D. James Dee

This site-specific work incorporated pieces of old vestments and canvas murals that were once on the wall of the church.

E

Jenifer Borg

Summer Evening

Dyed, drymounted, pieced; silk broadcloth; 30 by 40 inches. Photo: Hunter Clarkson

This work came from images I was using in traditional quiltmaking. Frustrated by the extensive time involved to complete a quilt, I began using the same hand-dyed silk from my quilts with dry-mount tissue on paper or mat board. Each piece is cut and fit together like a puzzle.

Although more literal images appear in this piece than my quilts, my continuing interest is in using pattern and color to suggest a sense of narrative related to time, landscape, or internal puzzles.

E

A

Susan Dahlberg

Jonheda Hamlet in Djura Parish, Dalarna

Appliqué, embroidery; cotton; 130 by 90 cm.

Even though I am autodidact, I have learned to dye fabric so that the colors are appealing.
I sew all seams twice, first with a loose tension, then with a tight one.

B

Barbara Head

Sailing

Machine appliqué and stitching; cotton, silk, synthetics; 54 by 46 inches.
Photo: John Melville

A

B

THREE DIMENSIONS

Dona J. Look

#904

Sewing, wrapping; white birch
bark; 10¾ by 10¾ inches.
Photo: Dedra Walls

A

B

A

Mimi Leutsch

Dance of Sun and Rain

Painting, dyeing, laminate construction; linen, wood, foam; 59 by 96 inches.

This folding screen was designed as a celebration of fiber—the horizontal and vertical panels interlocking as if they were woven together.

B

Marjorie Hoeltzel

VII Quilt Columns

Stitching, stripping; hardware cloth, fabric, clothing labels; 328 by 60 by 30 inches.
Photo: Dan Pearce

These were designed for the corporate offices of Edison Brothers stores in St. Louis. The fabric strips and labels are from the firm's lines of sportswear and shoes.

The piece is derived from the quilt pattern, Courthouse Steps.

C

Peque Canas

Untitled

Construction; lutradur, rayon.
Photo: Doug Van Zande

I work to integrate, as well as contrast, the piece with the surrounding space.

D

Dawn MacNutt

Kindred Spirits at Alderney Gate

Twining, casting; fisherman's rope, bronze; 56 to 74 inches high.

In the journey of life, we are sometimes alone, sometimes relating to one another. Whether we are at a distance or physically close to another human being we are all alone, and yet all related to a family—to one another.

C

D

147

A

Laurie Gross

Holocaust Memorial

Weaving, painting; linen, ink;
117 by 77 inches.
Photo: Paul Hester

*By sewing and manipulating
the painted threads, I reached
a point at which I felt as if I was
actually drawing with the
threads. My goal with the piece
was to impart a sense of hope
for the future as well as a sense
of despair over a tragic event in
our history.*

B

Myung hee OH

*The Monument of An Ancient
City*

Knotting, dyeing, painting;
Korean paper ("dak"), copper
wire, cord; 145 by 300 by 32 cm.

*Using varied materials, I am
expressing harmony and dis-
harmony.*

C

Sandy Webster

Offerings

Woven, layered, embedded,
painted; handwoven fabrics,
paper, clay, wood; 36 by 48
by 3 inches.
Photo: Jim Galbraith

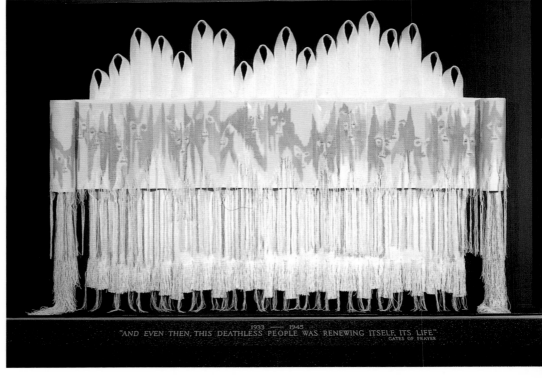

1933 —— 1945
"AND EVEN THEN, THIS DEATHLESS PEOPLE WAS RENEWING ITSELF, ITS LIFE"
GATES OF PRAYER

C

D

Peggy Loughlin DeBell
Alter/Altar Piece

Dyeing, painting; paper pulp, hardware cloth, cotton, wood; 50 by 78 by 6 inches.
Photo: Al Nuckols

Inspired by a pile of cut sticks on a roadside and by one of my favorite childhood pastimes: building teepees and lean-to's.

E

Lois Schklar
Standing Form

Laminate, machine and hand stitching; burlap, gesso, paint; 67 by 12 by 5 inches.
Photo: Peter Hogan

D

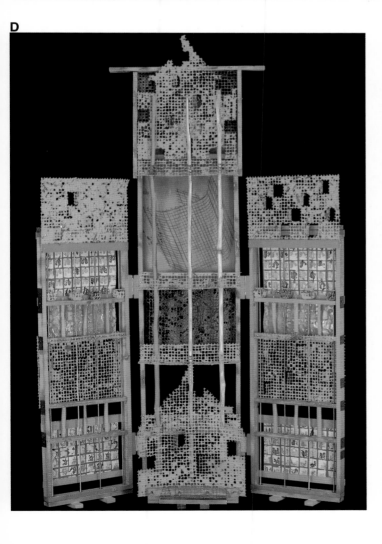

E

149

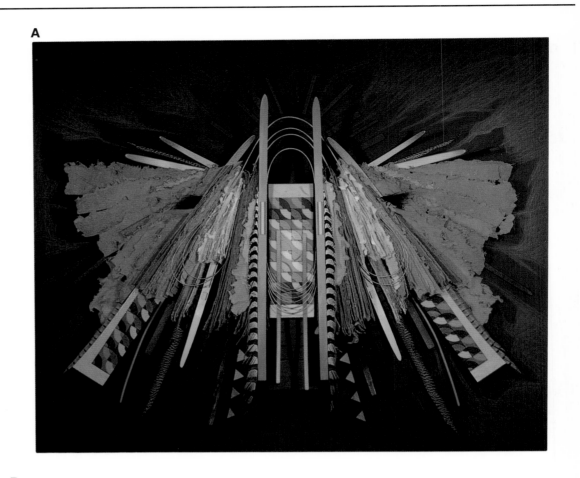

A

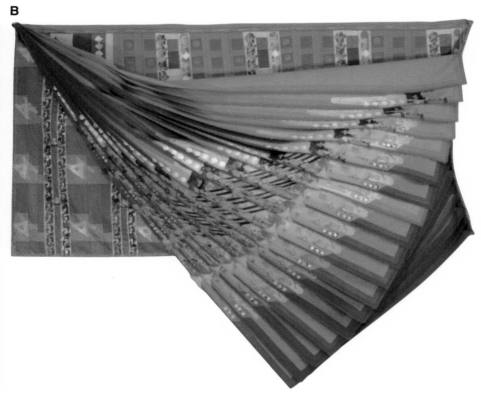

B

C

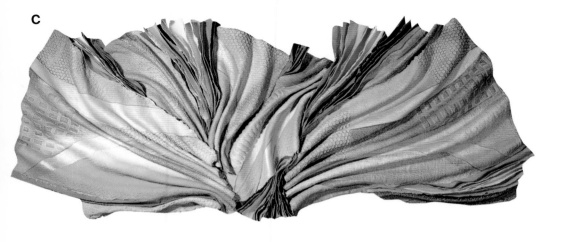

D

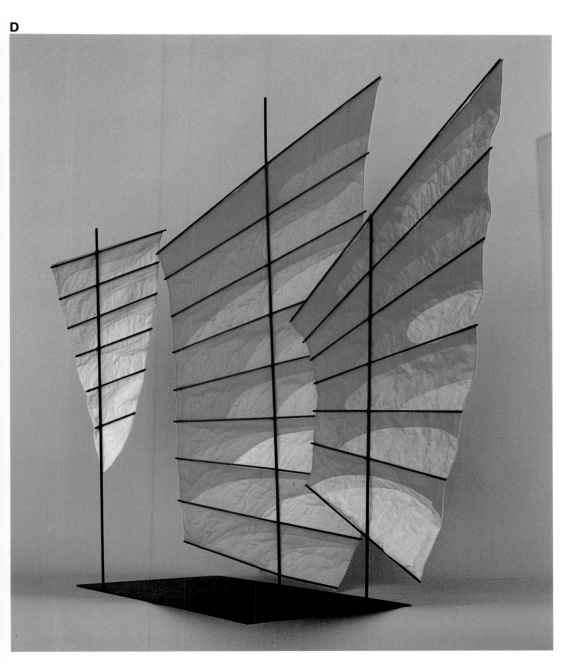

A

John Hubbard

Flight Forms IV

Construction; handmade paper, paint, hair, feathers, wood, styrofoam, colored pencil; 48 by 40 by 7 inches.

Amish quilts, North and South American Indian motifs influence my work.

B

Pamela Becker

Inside-Outside

Painting, piecing, appliqué, embroidery; cotton blends, textile paint, ribbon, metallics; 34 by 42 by 7 inches.

Layers of fabric are used to construct forms reminiscent of natural phenomenon. Stacked in a predetermined manner, the layers are manipulated by sewing or with rope to create the desired form. When the piece is hung on the wall, gravity exerts its pull on the layers. Each one folds over onto the one below, building up form and image.

C

Martha Chatelain

Sashay

Mold and deckle forming; handmade paper, Procion dye, acrylic paint, mica powders; 65 by 26 by 3 inches.
Photo: Susan Blanchard

D

Jo Olf

Sails I

Machine piecing, hand quilting, dyeing; cotton, cotton blends, Procion dye; 32 by 37 by 16 inches.

This quilt is part of a series of sails meant to express the freedom and direction I felt on returning to college.

A

Heidi Darr-Hope

Once Removed: Makura

Painting, collage, embroidery, quilting, burnishing; cotton, acrylic paint, ink, mulberry paper, wire, glass beads; 36 by 18 by 2 inches.

The work I create documents my travels—some real, some imaginary.

B

John Hawthorne

Ties That Bind

Embroidery, tapestry, beading; cotton, wool, beads, bronze; 24 by 21 by 12 inches.
Photo: Alice McCabe

C

Tracy Ruhlin

Grid Miniature #5

Tabby, assemblage; Procion dye, monofilament, mylar, straw; 9 by 12 inches.
Photo: Joe Thomas

D

Yael Bentovim

A View From My Window

Painting, assemblage; hand-made paper, paint; 8 by 6 by 8 inches.
Photo: Claire Curran

My work and my garden are both a constant source of wonder and pleasure for me.

E

Bettina Wurm

Wings

Cutting, dyeing, glueing; cotton, wire; 84 by 108 by 84 inches.

In the piece I tried to emphasize the lightness of the optical motion of color and form.

A

B

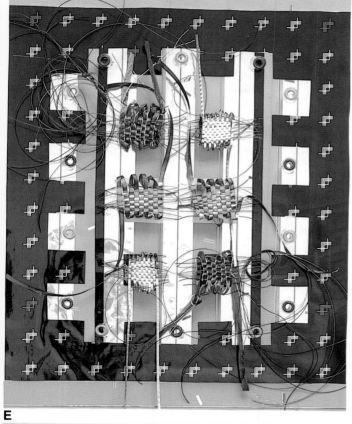

A

Renata Rozsivalova

Growing In The Cube

Bobbin lace; flax; 14 by 16 by 14 cm.

B

Irene Mudrova

Sick Eco Wind

Embroidery, heat lamination; plastic, yarn; 300 by 250 cm.

C

Maria Danielova

Optical Lace

Bobbin lace; linen, cotton, lace; 110 by 110 by 110 cm.

D

David Weidig

Trumple Tower

Random twill, assemblage; teletype paper, paint, medium, mylar, muslin; 26 by 72¼ inches. Photo: Mary Rezny

Inspired by the Trump empire and its glitz, the surface of this piece was crumpled to represent a gelatinous foundation and crumbling facade.

E

Joan Silver

Aegis IV

Construction; graphited needle-point mesh; 19½ by 45 inches.

My work has been influenced by medieval and Asian armour. The idea that one is protected and captured is a provocative duality.

F

Marie-Laure Ilie

Silent Chimes

Painting, assemblage; organza; 30 by 70 by 12 inches.

I am exploring the cocoon-like atmosphere of a room when it's sunny and the transparent curtains are drawn.

A

B

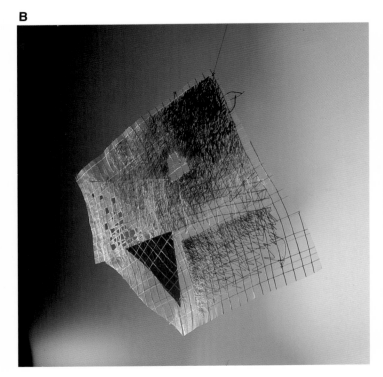

C

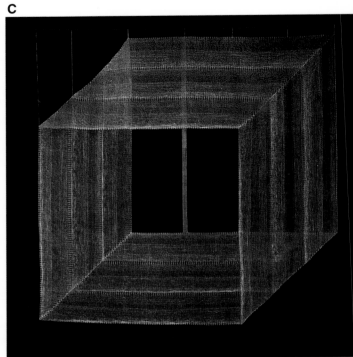

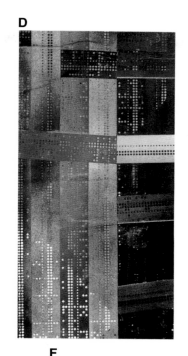

D

F

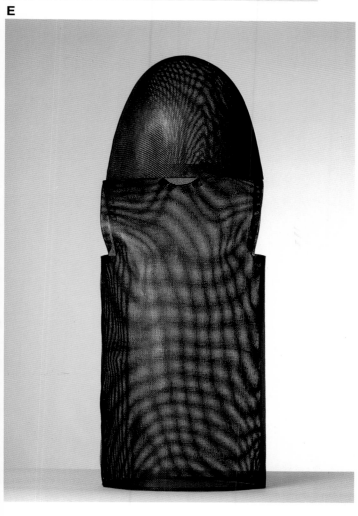

E

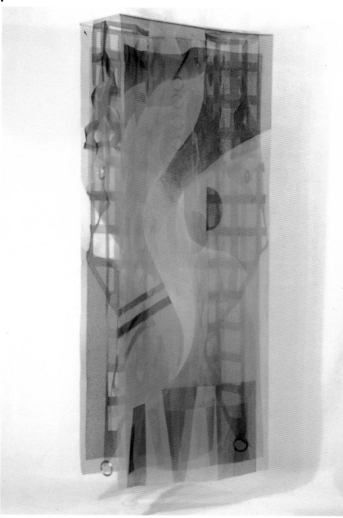

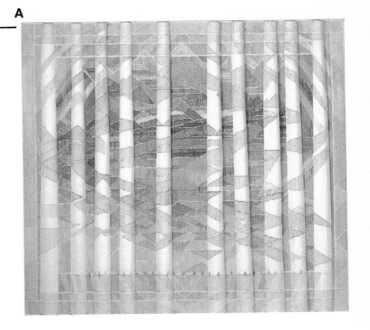

A

Kaija Sanelma Harris

On the Way to Shangri-La

Moorman technique; cotton, wool, silk; 63 by 59 by 2 inches. Photo: A. K. Photos, Grant A. Kernan

B

Kathleen Armstrong

Sun Units

Painted warp, weaving; linen, cotton; 20 by 10½ inches.

C

Stephanie Randall Cooper

Everyone Has A Story

Machine piecing, hand sewing; cotton, silk, foam rubber, canvas; 63 by 75 by 1½ inches each. Photo: Mark Frey

I wanted to abstractly suggest the concept of two sides to every story by creating two distinctly different designs. On one side the colors and shapes undulate smoothly and simply, while the other design contains chunky, hard-edged shapes with mismatched colors.

D

Holly Kenny

Horizon

Warp face technique, wrapped dowels; cotton, linen, wool, raffia; 52 by 30 inches. Photo: Jerry Anthony

I am interested in combining the elements of texture, design and color to create something that pleases the senses–an image to enjoy through sight and touch. But it is in color that I find the greatest means of expression. It is a powerful influence in our lives and it is that influence that I want to convey in my work: the emotional attachment we have to color.

E

Dora Hsiung

Red Cubes

Wrapping; English rug yarn, wood; 16 by 16 by 2⅛ inches.

Optical illusion plays an important role in my work. The squares appear to change continuously as one's perception shifts from horizontal to vertical.

F

Barbara Brown

Colour Patch-Shadow Patch

Knitting, assemblage; anodized aluminum, wire, wood; 95 by 135 by 5 cm.

Inspired by patchwork quilting, the background cloth is knitted and knitted patches are attached with one stitch.

B

C

D

E

F

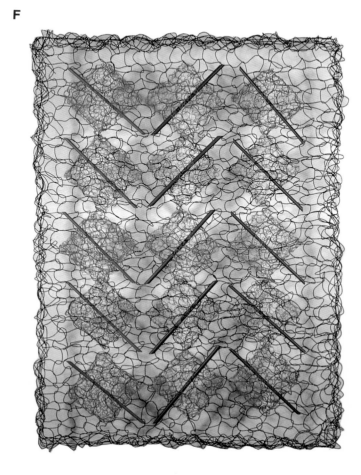

157

A

Marion Ongerth

Nine Rings

Shibori, machine pieced and quilted; dyed silk; 20½ by 61½ by 20½ inches.
Photo: Jonathan Reichek

This is a departure from my usual wall pieces. I am delighted with the shadows created as the piece slowly spins.

B

Theresa Baggett

Exit to the Inside: II

Double weave, huck pattern; mylar, ramie, plexiglass; 30 by 40 by 10 inches.
Photo: Gary Sutton

C

Jackie Abrams

Red Towers #2

Loom-woven panels, notched, lashed; dyed raffia, red osier dogwood, waxed linen; 14 by 20 by 11 inches.
Photo: John D. Goodman

D

Jean McWhorter

Ancient Song

Construction; canvas, acrylic, string, copper, brass, wood; 60 by 60 by 4 inches.

This piece consists of two sections: a top form and a background piece. The top section is a large formed shape with a knot-and-paint texture; hand plaited string with copper shapes and brass bells hang loosely from the bottom. I want my work to elicit emotions and to produce "visual sound" for the eyes.

A

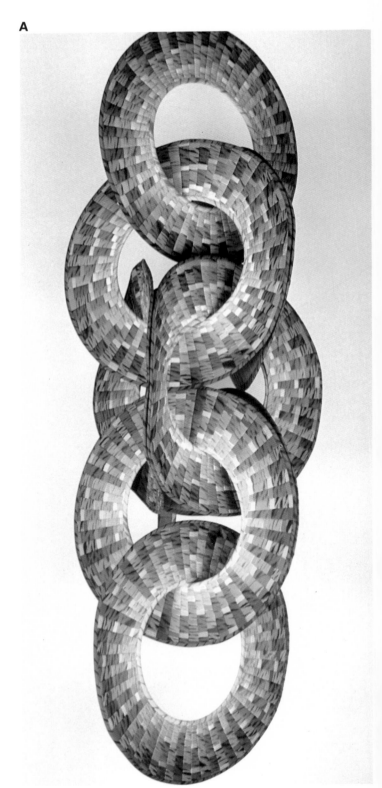

B

C

D

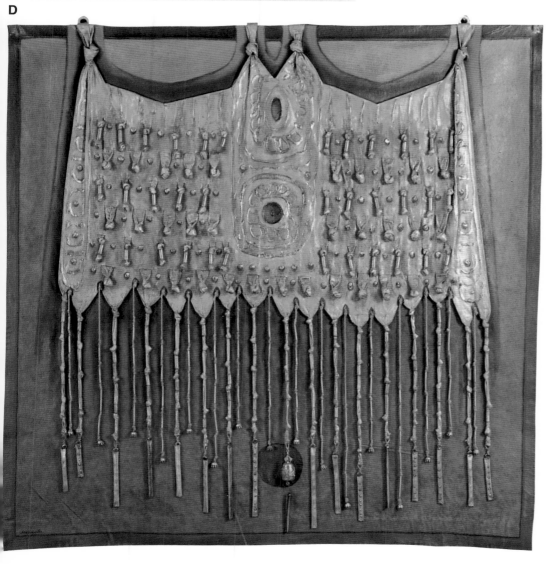

159

A

A

Michalene Groshek

Marsh Magic

Screen printing, stitching, sculpting, painting; cotton, dye, paint, wood; 14 by 30 by 12 inches.
Photo: University of Kansas Photo Services

The work describes dramatic moments in nature when atmospheric qualities, light and natural forms harmonically merge to create a "magical or mysterious" scene.

B

David McCarthy

Between Heaven and Earth

Basketry, weaving, wrapping, gold leaf; pine needles, feathers, porcupine quills, linen, raffia, cotton; 18 by 26 by 14 inches.
Photo: Joseph Jovanovich, Chicago

Baskets in my mixed media are most often human torsos.

C

Barbara Bate

Totem Vessel

Sheet formed, hand cast paper; cattail, abaca, waxed linen, brass, bronze slag, reeds; 12 by 16 by 10 inches.
Photo: Larry Booth

My work has evolved from two-dimensional, flat surfaces to having fibers and found objects. The found objects, or treasures as I like to call them, are an integral part of my work. I aim for them to give a heartbeat to it rather than merely be decorative.

D

Sherrill Hunnibell

Untitled Landscape With Catalyst Icon

Twining, stitching, mixed media construction; round and flat reed, wood, cotton, paint; 22 by 23 by 22 inches.
Photo: Marc Harrison

The idea of working with multiple form statements has always intrigued me. I enjoy the challenge of creating forms which first have to work well as complete entities individually, then as an integral part of a larger composition.

E

Rhonda Cunha

Holding Back The Lawn

Silkscreen, construction; fabric, wood, clay, glass, wire; 62 by 70 by 17 inches.

In seeking to realize both long- and short-term career goals, I have been compelled to relocate many times over the past decade. This constant moving has proven to be both fascinating and disillusioning. Though it has always been stimulating on a personal and artistic level, my travels have been at times lonely, draining, and have often left me with a sense of loss when I leave a place and people I love, as well as my anticipation of discovery as I arrive in a new place.
I use the lawn as a symbol of my desire for stability, yet there is my inability to achieve it because of my transient lifestyle.

B

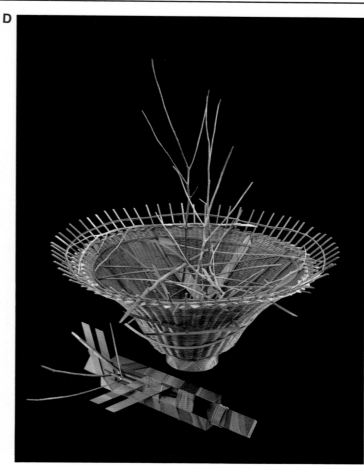

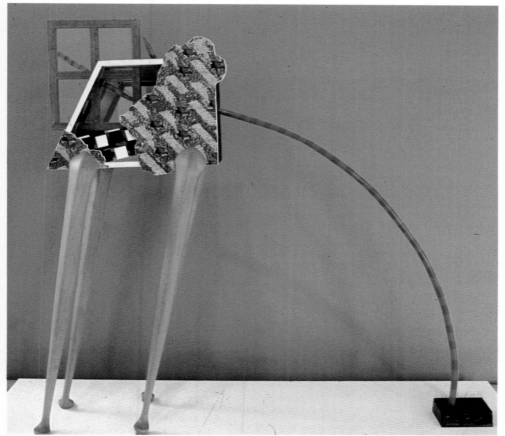

A

Susan Planalp

Blue Mesa Bowl

Handcast paper, loomed bead-work; handmade paper, beads; 16 by 16 by 3½ inches.
Photo: Todd Misk

My imagery and color come from studying Amish quilt colors and basket patterns of the Northwest Indian tribes.

B

Barbara Davis

Lava Idol

Woven, airbrushed; cast paper, hand-dyed reed, paint; 20 by 8 by 7 inches.
Photo: William Lenke

C

Ilse Bolle

Breakthrough

Lashing, twining; bamboo, raffia, rattan, handmade paper; 32 by 52 by 38 inches.

D

Lois Schklar

Offering Bowl

Laminate, machine and hand stitching; burlap, gesso, paint; 14 by 9 inches.
Photo: Peter Hogan

E

Donna Marie Fleming

Dagdha's Cauldron II

Fabric casting, appliqué, layering; metallic thread, cotton, acrylic; 13 by 10 inches.
Photo: Marona Photography

The quilt is always integral to my work. The nurturing aspect of this quilt is consistent with the vessel form. Using light and space as the batting element of construction, the piece has been strip layered and sewn.

F

Carolyn Golberg

Vessels

Watercolor, airbrush; cotton, abaca, handmade paper; 16 by 22 by 5 inches.
Photo: Christine Benkert

A

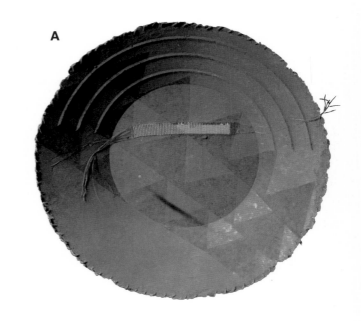

B

C

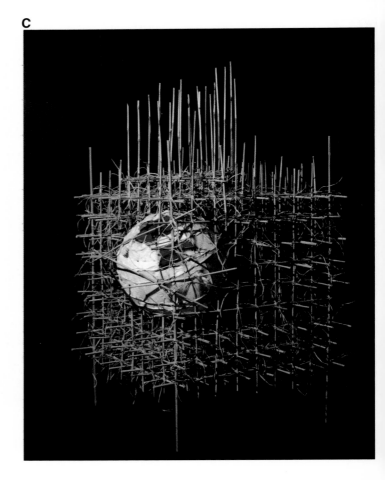

D

E

F

A

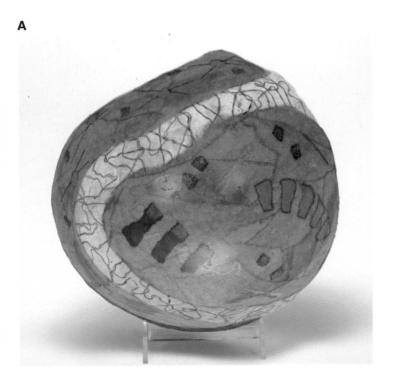

B

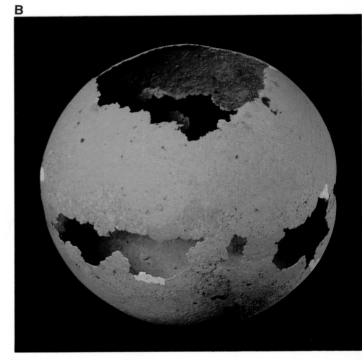

C

D

E

A

Marla Brill

Clambake

Molded handmade paper; abaca, kozo, waxed linen, dye; 9½ by 5½ inches.
Photo: Deborah Cartwright

B

Karen White

Birthday Bowl

Dyed, cast and sprayed paper pulp; handmade paper, aqueous dispersed pigments; 16 by 16 by 16 inches.
Photo: Boyd B. Burkhart

Containers have always held a fascination for me. They hold creativity, emotions, desires and visions.

C

Nicole Dextras

The Noodles I Would Make For You Boys

Cast paper, Xerox transfer; cotton pulp, dyes, pencil; 16 inches high.

D

Bird Ross

Make Adjustments Before Cutting

Sewing; rayon, paper; 11 by 12 by 11 inches.
Photo: Charles Frizzell

E

Bird Ross

Big Blue Bowl

Sewing; cotton; 26 by 6 by 26 inches.
Photo: Charles Frizzell

A

Molly Hart

Sea Pod

Weaving; copper, aluminum, mylar, wire, plastic tubing; 28 by 13 by 20 inches.

An abstraction of the human form, this represents openness, radiance, receptivity and protection.

B

Mona Roseland

Sea Urchin Basket

Plain weave; reed; 22 by 16 inches.
Photo: Dan Batchlor, Fine Photography

C

John F. McGuire

Casaba

Plaiting, surface embellishment; black ash, rosa rugosa, leather; 9 by 9 inches.

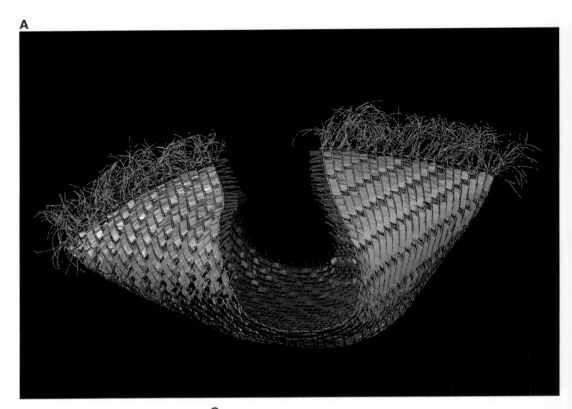

D

E

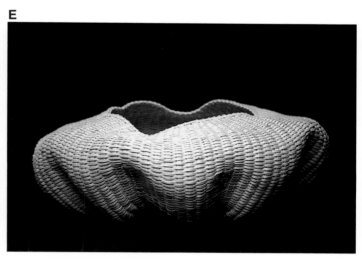

F

D

Jill Montague

Journeyman

Plaiting; flat reed, raffia; 54 by 24 by 18 inches.
Photo: Ron B.

Working with basketry through a combination of forms has allowed me to utilize the concept of vessel as the foundation for the sculptural form I am pursuing.

E

Judith Olney

Ripple

Stake and strand weaving; red maple; 13 inches dia. by 6½ inches.
Photo: Roger D. Olney

F

Sue Smith

Ti Twined Basket

Twining; palm seed stems, willow, waxed linen; 12 by 12 inches.

The gathering process is an important factor of my basket-making. Nature not only provides the vast majority of my materials, but also is the inspiration behind my work. Basketmakers weave a little of themselves and their environment in their baskets, making them as unique as the person who made them.

A

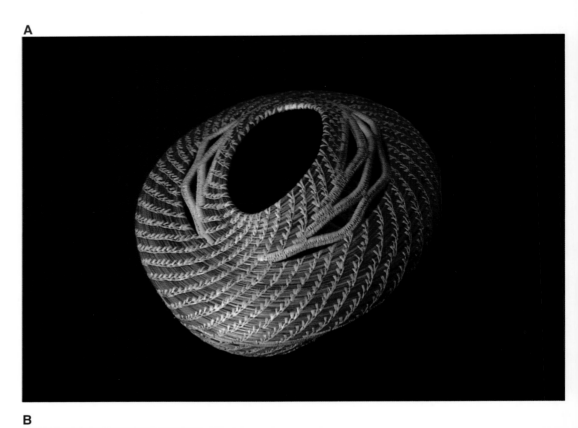

B

A
Marilyn Moore

Resistance

Coiling, wrapping; pine needles, raffia; 11 by 8 by 11 inches.
Photo: John Moore

B
Char Wiss

Timeprints II

Coiling; waxed linen, acrylic-coated rush; 15½ by 10 by 15½ inches.
Photo: Mary A. Root

C
Priscilla Henderson

Bowl on Checked Wedge

Wickerweave, airbrush, lacquering; rattan; 22 by 12½ by 22 inches.
Photo: Lee Henderson

D
Kari Lonning

Geometry

5 rod wale, tapestry techniques; rattan; 18½ by 12 inches.

I use a weaving technique where four strands of rattan are woven sequentially to create the "fabric" of the walls, and a form of tapestry to weave in specific designs. To create weight, both actual and implied, I developed a double-walled construction.

In keeping with my Scandinavian heritage, I work in a subdued palette.

A
Flo Hoppe
UB46

Twining, lashing; dyed rattan, waxed linen; 17 by 6½ inches.
Photo: John C. Keys

B
Maggie Henton
Square box, round lid

Plaiting, weaving; dyed rattan, telephone wire; 14 by 12½ inches.

My early training was in constructed textiles, and this background continues to have a strong influence on my work.

C
Carol Eckert
Cloud Dragon

Coiling; cotton, metallic filament; 5½ by 7 by 5 inches.
Photo: Ross Miller

D
Ellen Clague
If Wishes Were Horses

Coiling, collage, blown paper; raffia, handmade paper, beads, paint; 6 by 10 inches.

E
Jeannine Goreski
On The Edge

Bead netting; glass beads, nylon thread; 3 by 4¾ inches.
Photo: Rick Lucas

Beads are vehicles. They connote the precious and command close inspection revealing structure, line, image, color, light, and tactile sensuality.

Each bead is locked in a structured, ordered brick pattern. This bead-by-bead building process is important; it speaks of time, vulnerability, frailty, and integral elements.

F
Zoe Morrow
Ten Buck Two Bag

Twill and plain weave, sewing; shredded U.S. currency, thread; 8 by 9 by 7½ inches.
Photo: Charles H. Jenkins III

Money is both material and statement. I want the viewer to re-think his/her relationship to money. It's not how much you have, it's what you do with it.

A

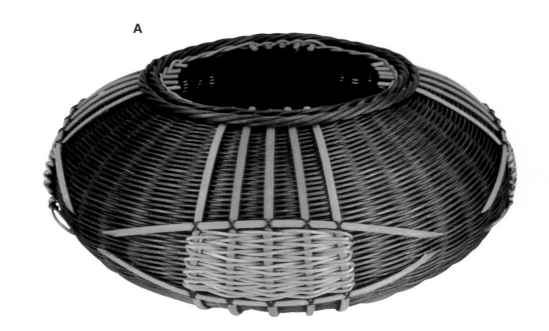

B

C

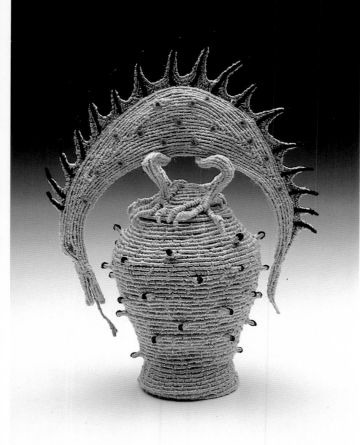

D

E

F

A

Sue Fedenia

Am I Blue?

Mariposa, knot stitch, coiling;
painted reed, waxed linen;
13 by 4 by 13 inches.
Photo: Jeff Stanley

*When I discovered waxed linen,
plain reed, and the mariposa
knot stitch, I was roaming
around the Southwest: from
Denver to Santa Fe, then to
Arizona. In fact it was basketry
that led me to Arizona my first
winter—the desire to hike the
desert and do my baskets. While
there I began pushing the baskets further, first by doing the
mariposa with three knots, thus
making them more open and
translucent; then by adding color.*

*I've enjoyed playing with the
colors and their effects on each
other and, lately, the interplay of
layers of baskets.*

B

Gina Jalakas

Solitude

Coiling; paper, waxed linen;
17½ by 15 inches.
Photo: Georg Kase

*Coiling with waxed linen is ever
so slow. It is, however, wonder-
fully meditative and peaceful.*

C

Jane Lunow

In A Big Mud Puddle

Pyro engraving, dyeing, stitching;
gourd, dyes, enamel, pine
needles, waxed linen; 11 by
8½ by 11 inches.
Photo: Roger Olney.

*This was inspired by contemplat-
ing ordinary puddles after a
storm. The puddles had delicate
leaves in them which had been
sprinkled with mica.*

D

Patti Lechman

Gauri

Knotting; dye, nylon; 6 by 5 by
3¼ inches.

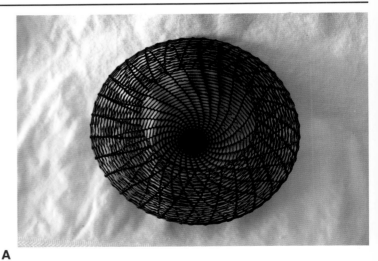

A

B

C

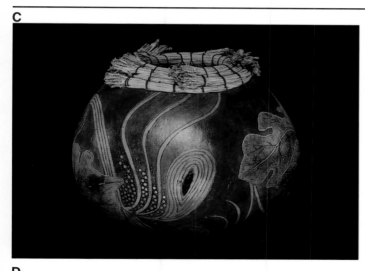

D

A

Mary E. Irvine

Citadel

Plaiting, twining; cedar bark and root; 4 by 12½ by 3½ inches.

The base, side panels and spokes are the same piece of bark and remain joined together at the base.

B

Sharon Robinson

Burble

Coiled pine needles, linen cord; 4 inches high.

I love form, color and texture, in that order.

Deborah Banyas
The Serpentines

Sewing, painting; cotton, acrylic
paint, beads; 48 by 41 by 11½
inches.
Photo: John Seyfried

*The form and subject of my work
springs from my love of animals
and folk art.*

A

A

Jane Burch Cochran

The Last Dance

Machine piecing, hand appliqué; fabric, beads, buttons, paint, sequins, glitter, cheesecloth; 69 by 79 inches.
Photo: Pam Mofort

While looking through a bag of rags, I discovered an old dress made from cheesecloth. Since I use painted canvas as background for my quilts, I applied a thin coat of gesso to adhere the dress to the canvas. I decorated it with buttons, beads and paint. I felt like the birds and mice from "Cinderella" who turned her plain dress in to one for the ball.

B

Tammy Lavanty

Emma and her Basket of Joy

Machine stitching and embroidery; silk, velvet, paint, beads, crystals; 12 by 23 inches.
Photo: Tom Griffen

I get pleasure and fulfillment in the world of fantasy, magic and whimsy. It is a playful and uncomplicated place which inspires me to create creatures like Emma.

C

Lenore Davis

Work Sock Dancers

Stuffing, sewing, painting; linen, polyester, textile paint, colored pencils; 15 inches high.

These figures celebrate socks, clownish movements and symmetry, three of my favorite elements.

D

Kate Fiebing Piskor

Vladimir

Trapunto; muslin, dyed yarn, fiberfill; 18 by 72 by 12 inches.
Photo: John Robert Williams

I've had plenty of jobs, from menial labor to computer work, but now I'm living a dream. I've never had so much fun. I have a tremendous amount of eight-year-old left in me and I never want to lose it.

E

Linda Theede

I See London, I See France...

Painting, sewing, embellishing; fabric, yarn, lace, beads, feathers; 8 by 12 by 9 inches.

B

C

D

E

A
R. Renee Sherrer
Brassiere Prom Dress #2

Sewing; brassieres, gloves, net.

The impetus for my work is taking everyday things, thinking about their meaning in relationship to my experiences, and creating something which expresses my thoughts. What does it mean to know that I will have an engineered garment strapped to my chest for the rest of my life?

B
Robin White-Sieber
Armored Apron II

Quilting, batik, silkscreen; cotton, dye, lamé, netting; 36 by 60 by 2½ inches.

This is one of a series of non-wearable garments based upon the structure of armor. The apron is a visual metaphor which represents the dichotomy of protection and danger inherent in taking on a social role as an identity.

C
Carolyn Prince Batchelor
Mirror Dress

Embroidery, braiding; paper, paint, waxed linen thread; 25 by 29 inches.

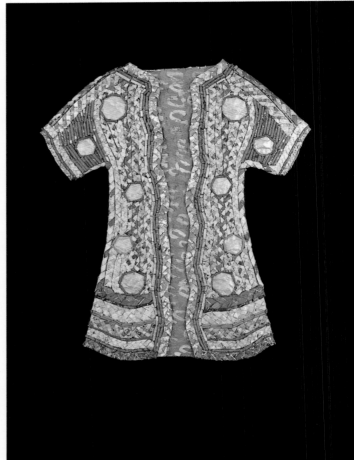

D

Ludmila Fintorova
Clown
Sewing; textiles, feathers; 30 by 30 cm.

E

Connie Lehman
secrets, amelia
Russian needlepunch, beading; silk, beads, sequins; 5 by 4⅜ inches.

F

Deborah Felix
Love of Objects
Painting, reverse appliqué, sewing; canvas, paint, pastels, vinyl, fabric; 228 by 72 inches.
Photo: Alan Watson

A

Anne Morrell

Tossed Salad

Machine appliqué, dyeing, piecing, embroidery, quilting; cotton; 57 by 66 inches.

My roots are in the living-off-the-land movement. I believe in combining the best of traditional and modern ideas and methods.

B

Kathy Wosika

Buried With the Baggage

Collage, construction; handmade paper, mulberry bark; 32½ by 21 by 2½ inches.
Photo: E. Z. Smith

My current work explores the death-transformation-ascension-rebirth cycle.

C

Nancy Martineau

Winkie

Traditional rug hooking; wool, wool blends; 30 by 23 inches.
Photo: Jed Eli

After experimenting with different fiber techniques, I've settled into my life as a rug hooker. This technique allows complete spontaneity of design. Each loop is independent of the next and most of my work is not planned.

D

Jacqueline Treloar

Le Cirque

Painting, marbling; Duppioni and organza silk, canvas, ribbon, braid, beads, sequins, paint; 84 by 84 inches.
Photo: Allison Oulette

The main drawing illustrates the Cirque de Soleil artists of Montreal. The borders of the piece represent the origins from which the circus has evolved; the court pageant with its jesters and buffoons, the theater of mime and drama, and the masks of tragedy and comedy.

The colors are light resistant pigment. The back is lined with a painted canvas for added durability and to allow the hanging to be seen from both sides.

A

B

C

D

A

B

C

A

Kyoung Ae Cho

Slides & Box

Tapestry; silk, cotton; slides: 2 by 2 inches, box: 2¼ inches.

B

Kathryn Pellman

Surfing L.A.

Piecing, appliqué, quilting; cotton, wool, silk; 117 by 89 inches.
Photo: Sharon Risedorph

A commentary on today's businessman and life in the fast lane.

C

Ira Ono

Pendant

Assemblage; porcelain, silk, found objects; 2½ by 2½ inches.
Photo: George Post

D

Peggy Moulton

Guard Pussies

Stacked fabric, embroidery; cotton, synthetics; 12 by 14 by 2 inches.
Photo: Kirby Moulton

I enjoy the challenge of putting unlike patterns and colors side by side. The fabric is left raw-edged and the embroidery is simple to convey spontaneity.

E

Jacque Parsley

Meeting of the Ladies Auxiliary

Sewing, couching, appliqué; hats, pearls, earrings, gloves.
Photo: Patrick Pfitser

F

Kathleen Franck-Quarterman

Just Another Snake In The Grass

Dyeing, gold leaf; silk; 80 by 36 by 2 inches.

The piece contains two free-hanging panels, one behind the other.

D

E
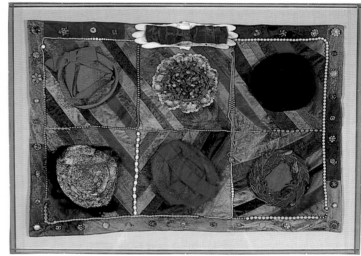

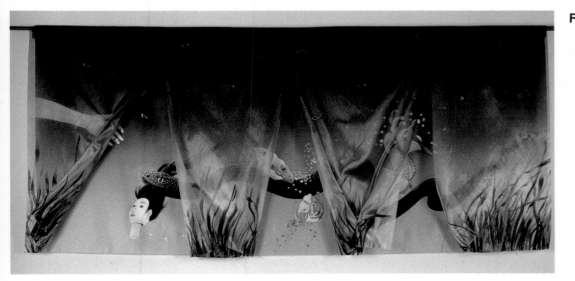

F

A
Diane Burchard

Capote Dos

Assemblage; hand-dyed paper, feathers, acrylic paint, linen, wood, plexiglas; 10 by 18 by 10 inches.
Photo: Lightworks, Santa Fe, New Mexico

B
Wendy Huhn

Bessie, Bossie, Flo & A Friend Visit Georgia's Sky Above the Clouds

Machine pieced, hand quilted and painted; cotton, fabric paint, color laser transfers; 27½ by 38½ inches.

One in a series of my traveling cows and their adventures as they explore the world. Georgia O'Keefe has been a great inspiration to me. This is the girls' third visit to Georgia's.

C
Kate Martin

Little Glimpses

Punched hooked rug; wool, cotton; 33 by 90 inches.
Photo: Joe Coca

This piece was inspired by my mother who reads tea leaves.

D
Anna Cinzerova-Pantikova

I

Bobbin lace; flax; 33 by 33 cm.

E
Jacqueline Govin

La rougeole

Patchwork, appliqué, embroidery, painting; cotton, silk, metallic threads, lace, paint; 19 by 27 cm.
Photo: Wolters

F
Barbara Watler

She's Barking Up the Wrong Tree

Machine quilting and sewing; cotton, cotton blends, paint; 52 by 101 inches.
Photo: Doug Shaw

This is my tribute to women who are now, and have always been, willing to take risks, even though it sometimes turns out we're barking up the wrong tree.

C

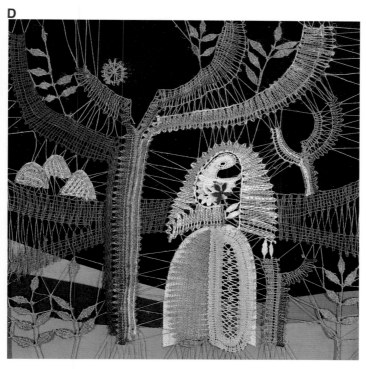

D

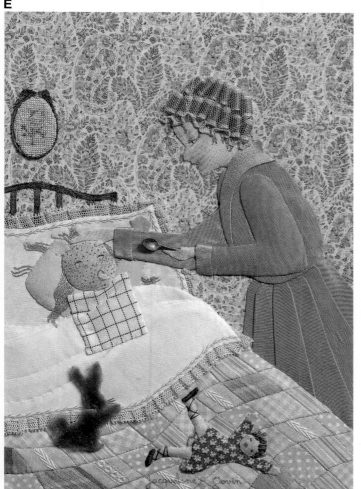

E

F

A

Sheila O'Hara

I Go For The Juggler

Warp faced pickup; silk, linen, lurex; 25¾ by 14¾ inches.

The weaving was inspired by the Cirque du Soleil, a Canadian circus which has toured the U.S. for a few years. It was a great show, like nothing I have ever seen.

B

Sylvia Ptak

In the Corner of the Attic

Collage; color Xerox, commercial fabric, handwoven wire; 77 by 44 inches.
Photo: Henry Feather

A

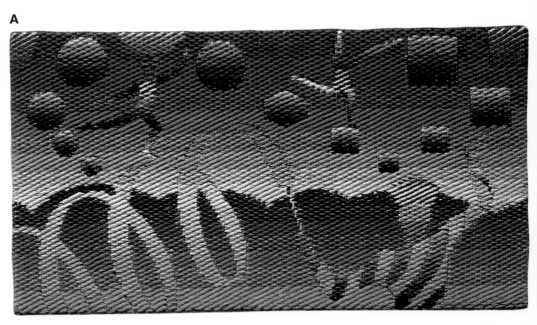

B

186

SURFACE DESIGN

Lenore Davis

Everyday Saints

Monotype, painting; cotton,
textile paint; 44 by 44 inches.

*This piece grew from a single
block into the figure grouping
that prompted the title. The
gestural attitudes and the gold
pigment remind me of paintings
of saints.*

A

Martha Desposito

Prom Night

Drawing, painting; fabric, acrylic, pastel, oil stick; 40 by 51½ inches.
Photo: Richard Bram

Inspired by a 1962 photo of me getting ready for the prom.

B

Nancy Erickson

Rabbits Search the Asteroids for Healthy Habitat

Machine stitching and quilting; velvet, satin, cotton, paint; 44 by 24 inches ea.

C

Deborah Kirkegaard

Statue Series III: On her 30th birthday she signed a contract with Statuesque Perfume

Silk screen, collage, painting; cotton, acrylics; 23¾ by 14 inches.
Photo: Jeremy Jones

I saw this statue in a backyard in the Portuguese district of Toronto. I jumped the fence and photographed her.

D

Martha Desposito

The Fat Cats

Drawing, painting; fabric, acrylic, pastel, oil stick; 40 by 50 inches.
Photo: Richard Pram

A

B

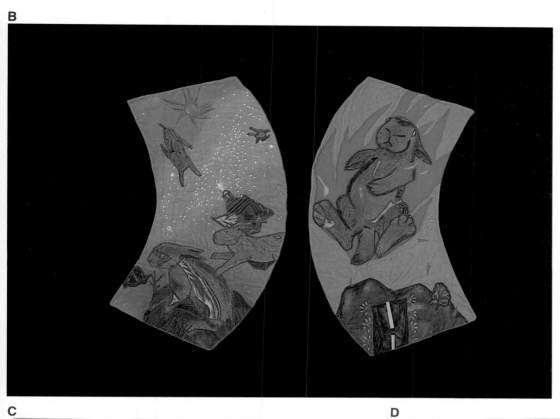

C

D

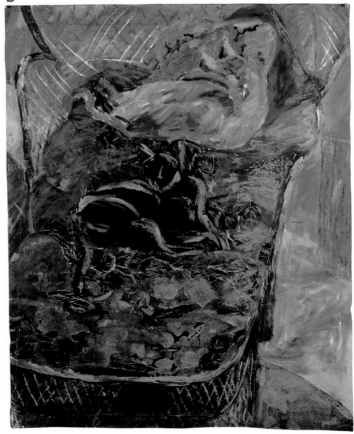

189

A

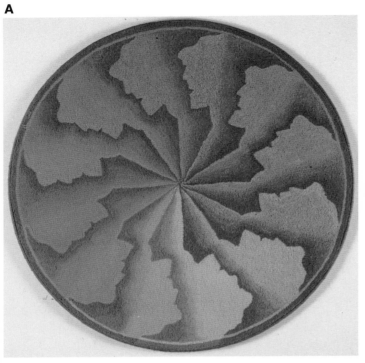

B

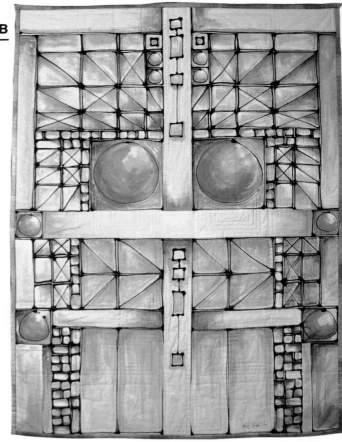

C

D

F

A

Peg Irish

The Old Man

Dyed, hand hooked; wool flannel, cotton; 24 inches, diam.
Photo: Andrew Edgar

B

Gerry Chase

Ascension

Machine piecing and quilting, painting; cotton, India ink, acrylic paint; 36 by 49 inches.

In this piece I am playing with the idea of architectural forms (by their nature, very stationary) gaining buoyancy.

C

Marie-Laure Ilie

Sweet Blues

Painted, fused, sewn; nylon mesh, textile paint; 67 by 96 by 7 inches.

The personality of this fabric lends itself to technical explorations and variations of shapes and colors. The transparency factor is especially alluring and adds a dimension of mystery.

D

Pamela Matiosian

Dialogue

Dyed, pieced, quilted; silk, kozo, felt, pine, gold leaf; 78 by 156 by 8 inches.
Photo: Ruyell Ho

This piece was commissioned for a building whose architecture was strongly influenced by Frank Lloyd Wright. My work was a response to that.

E

Linda Levin

Siena: Paese Dei Sogni

Dyeing, machine stitching; Procion dye; 70 by 55 inches.
Photo: Louise Webber

F

Sine McCann

Discoveries

Stitching, painting; paper, gouache, pastels, foil; 60 by 80 by 5 cm.

From research undertaken in the Red Desert in Australia.

B

C

A

Marna Goldstein Brauner

Agnese

Photo-silkscreen, stamping, painting, appliqué, stitching; linen, silk, dye, pigments, beads; 61 by 46 inches.
Photo: Mary Jo Tole

This is my homage to St. Agnes, a martyr who was sainted because she wouldn't catch on fire when they tried to burn her at the stake.

B

Dana Boussard

High Tump in Autumn

Appliqué, painting; canvas, cotton, velvet; 54 by 64 inches.
Photo: Stan Raifel

C

Susan Mosler

Island

Painted, beaded, embroidered, machine and hand quilted; cotton, fiber paint, beads; 58 by 55 inches.

D

Jacqueline Treloar

The Return of Ulysses

Painting, appliqué, stitching; Duppioni and organza silk, cotton, beads, ribbons; 88 by 66 inches.

The piece illustrates the return home of Ulysses, and the slaughtering of the pretenders to his throne.

The top areas are images heat-transferred onto terylene. Ribbons are silk organza and translucent polyester. Light can pass through these areas; the solid silk areas are backed with cotton for protective purposes.

D

D

E

A
Linda DeLuca
Untitled
Gouache; 32 by 27 cm.

B
Cecile Blenke
Rondo
Gutta resist, painting; silk, Procion dye; 20 by 26 inches.

C
Martha Vick Robbins
Untitled
Batik; silk; 36 by 144 inches.

D
Sally Weatherill
Rooster's Nightmare
Silkscreen; velveteen; 60 by 36 inches.

E
Patresha Mandel
Projection
Silkscreen, painted; burlap, dyes, fiber paints, crayons; 108 by 156 inches.
Photo: Marti Thurman

Like the Surrealists who looked to Freud, and the Abstract Expressionists who looked to the unconscious, I am attracted to understanding my personal symbolism.

My work embodies a primitive mola-like bird image. A bird can be viewed as a symbol of transcendence, a release from a confining pattern of existence.

A

Sandra Sider

Eyes of Egypt

Photography, stamp printing, machine piecing; cotton, cyanotype, fabric paint; 36 by 39½ inches.
Photo: Roberto Sandoval

B

Sylvia Ptak

Recollections

Collage, photo transfer; line, cotton, handwoven wire; 100 by 69 inches.
Photo: Henry Feather

C

Kathy Weaver

Soweto Suite, Part One— Imprisoned

Silk screen, piecing, machine quilting; cotton; 76 by 76 inches.
Photo: Nelson Armour

D

Becky Schaefer

Normal Interest

Machine pieced, Xerox transfer; crepe acetate, cotton; 26 by 21 inches.

The image is from Bill Owen's Suburbia.

E

Tatiana Krizova Lizon

Together

Art protis, collage, stitching; wool fleece, fabric, threads; 27 by 49 inches.
Photo: Peter Lizon

F

Teresa Barkley

Peacock Plaid

Machine piecing, hand appliqué, quilting, heat-transferred photo; cotton, rayon, acrylic paint; 53 by 69 inches.
Photo: Bakal-Schwartzberg Studio

A

B

C

D

E

F

A
Claudia Lee
Daven's Birthday

Hand manipulated paper pulp,
surface design; cotton linters,
dyes and ink; 16 by 15 inches.
Photo: Joe Muncey

B
Linda MacDonald
Amphora

Airbrush, painting, dyeing, stitching; cotton, embroidery floss,
dye, paint; 78 by 77 inches.

*The search for symbol, object,
figure and message through
fabric, paint and stitchery is
an ongoing interest.*

C
Gabi Kessel
Wall Carpet

Painting; crepe de chine; 138 by
180 cm.

*I was an architecture student
and the main emphasis of my
work is on planning and design.
Stylistic elements, color harmony
and composition, principally of
the modern classical painters,
inspire my fabrics.*

D
Gudrun Lemb and Elke Weiler
Batman in New York

Painting (G. Lemb), appliqué,
quilting (E. Weiler); silk; 107 by
107 cm.

E
Judith Geiger
At the West's

Painting, gutta resist; China silk,
dye; 30 by 42 inches.
Photo: UCSB Photo Services

F
Betsy Sterling Benjamin
Sacred Places: Canyon

Wax resist; silk, kinsai gold
powder, acid dye; 90 by 120 cm.
Photo: Ito

A

B

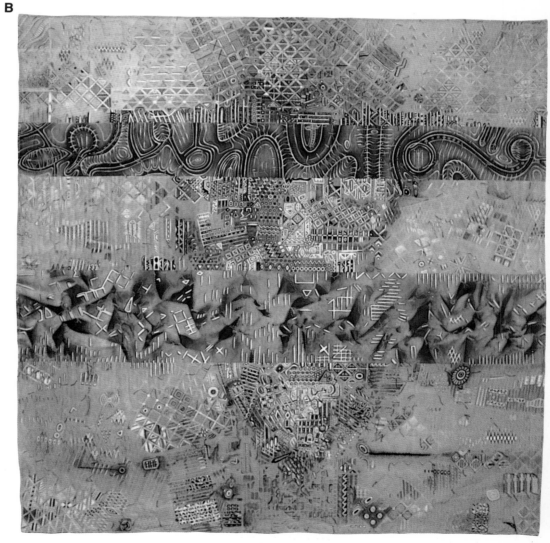

C

D

E

F

A

B

C

D

A

Amanda Richardson

Golden Grasses

Richardson-Tapestry; dye, textiles, adhesive; 78 by 66 inches. Photo: Roger Schreiber

B

Arnelle Dow

The Leaded Window

Batik; linen, fiber reactive dye; 40 by 36 by 2 inches. Photo: Tony Walsh

C

Mary Jo Stroh

Wotten Wabbit

Batik, screenprint, piecing, appliqué, quilting; cotton, cotton blends, rayon; 50 by 54 inches.

This quilt depicts the ongoing war between my gardener/ husband and his wily foe, the rabbit.

D

Linda France and David Hartge

Canned Peas

Hand painted using gutta resist; silk crepe de chine, French dyes; 30 by 30 inches.

Lynnie Wonfor

Secret Garden

Painted; silk, Procion dye,
ribbon; 46 by 46½ inches.

*This grew from an inspiration in
my garden when the fireweed
was in full bloom and bees were
visiting it from everywhere. The
center panel secretly opens to
reveal a painted beehive.*

A

INDEX